A YEAR OF IDEAS

365 sets of writing prompts and exercises

PATSY COLLINS

Copyright ©2021 Patsy Collins

All rights reserved.
The content of this book is subject to copyright. It may not be copied or transmitted in any way without the permission of the copyright holder, except for brief quotes used in reviews.

The author can be found at
www.patsycollins.co.uk
ISBN: 978-1-914339-00-4

Contents

Introduction..1
FAQs..2
How do I use this book?...2
How do I find today's prompt?...2
Which type of prompt should I choose?......................................2
How exactly do I turn an idea into a story?.................................3
Can I switch my character's gender?..4
Did I misunderstand the prompt?...4
Do I really have to write every day?...5
Can I submit work based on an idea in this book?......................5
1st January..7
10th January..10
20th January..13
1st February..18
10th February..21
20th February..24
1st March...28
10th March..31
20th March..34
1st April...39
10th April..42
20th April..45
1st May..49
10th May...52
20th May...55
1st June..60

10th June	63
20th June	66
1st July	70
10th July	73
20th July	76
1st August	81
10th August	84
20th August	87
1st September	92
10th September	95
20th September	98
1st October	102
10th October	105
20th October	108
1st November	113
10th November	116
20th November	119
1st December	123
10th December	126
20th December	129
A few reminders	133

Introduction

Hi, I'm Patsy Collins. I've been writing for most of this century. In that time I've completed six novels, co-written *From Story Idea to Reader* (an accessible guide to writing fiction) and produced twenty collections of themed short stories, averaging two dozen per book. Hundreds and hundreds of my short stories have been published – mainly in women's magazines such as My Weekly, The People's Friend, Woman's Weekly, Fiction Feast, The Weekly News, Ireland's Own, Allas … You get the point.

My work (fiction, non-fiction and poetry) has been placed in writing competitions. I've written articles, mostly about writing. In addition, I've run a blog for several years. Womagwriter.blogspot has official guidelines and information useful to those writing fiction for women's magazines. There are also regular links to free to enter writing competitions, guest posts from writers both new and established, technical details about self publishing and lots of other writing related stuff.

The thing these pieces of writing have in common is that they all started with an idea. Sometimes it was no more than a memory, phrase or situation. I built on that. Occasionally the words would flow quite easily, other times it felt I had to wrestle each one to the ground and nail it to my document. Usually the process was somewhere in between. I added words and sentences to my initial idea and over a period of hours, days, weeks or years created the finished product.

As you've probably gathered, ideas generally come easily to me. That isn't the case for all writers – and even those who rarely struggle with inspiration have periods when we just can't think about what to write next. It doesn't matter at all how easily the ideas come, nor where you get them from. The important thing is what you do next. Write it down (or type it out, or record on your phone, dictate to your secretary …) and then, every chance you get, add to it until you have your story.

Whether you're a new writer, or a more experienced one temporarily out of ideas, have hours to fill or just five free minutes, you'll find something in this book to help get you started – every day of the year.

FAQs

Of course there aren't really any frequently asked questions for this book as I'm writing this before it's published – but I haven't entirely made them up. Having presented workshops, and attended them myself, I'm aware of the types of questions which crop up when people are presented with writing exercises. And although it's a while since I was a new writer, I do remember something of how that felt.

How do I use this book?

The short answer is – however you like.

Use any part of any entry to write anything at all. Use them on your own, with a writing buddy, or in your writing group.

If you like to write every day choose the prompts for today's date. If you write less frequently (or wish to create multiple pieces a day) do each in turn. You can even pick something at random. The important thing is to decide on one quickly and give it a go. Don't go back to Facebook, stare at the ceiling, phone a friend, or anything else, until you've at least jotted down your first thoughts or completed the short exercise.

How do I find today's prompt?

In the contents list I've provided the page numbers for the 1st, 10th and 20th of each month. They're in chronological order, so once you're in the right third of the correct month, just flick through a couple of pages to the one you want.

Which type of prompt should I choose?

You have several options. (Sorry not to give many simple, definite answers, but writing is like that – there is no single right way.)

The 'Prompt' word or phrase is for free writing. Ideally use it without looking at the exercises below. Just write whatever comes to mind and don't worry if you start to go off topic. If you're very lucky this will morph into a story. More likely you'll end up deleting a lot of it – but you'll still be left with something to work on and expand. Alternatively use it to map out (plot) an idea for a story first, then start writing knowing where you're headed.

If you only have a few minutes, free write using the prompt for a timed period or attempt the quick exercise. Two minutes is enough for most of them, but if you have longer then keep going as long as you like.

If you have more time then use the story/scene suggestion – either with or without completing the short exercise first. If the short exercise gives you an idea that's different from my suggestion then go with it; you can always use mine another time. Alternatively just spend longer free writing to the prompt.

Whichever method you use, try to keep writing until you've got a rough draft finished and only then go back to correct any mistakes.

How exactly do I turn an idea into a story?

By writing!

I know that's simplistic, but it's true. It will take trial and error to work out the specifics of the method which works best for you, but beginning with writing down your initial thoughts is an excellent approach. Once you have something written it's easier to continue. Much easier.

Once you've recorded everything which immediately came to you, there are two main options. You may wish to leave it for a while and think carefully about what you'll write next, or you may prefer to get straight on with expanding the idea.

Approaches to consider are brainstorming, snowflake method and mind mapping. You'll find more information on these online and much more about the entire writing process in *From Story Idea to Reader*, written by myself and Rosemary J. Kind.

Keep asking questions of yourself, and your characters. 'Why?', 'who?' and 'what if?' are excellent ones. Consider which characters have most at stake and why each of them, including minor characters, behave as they do.

Once you've written all you can, leave this rough draft for a time. It's a good idea to work on something else before you come back to it. Read through what you've written and decide which parts can be strengthened, where you need to add more detail or information, and if there are sections which would be better cut. Be as honest and ruthless as you can bear to be.

You may find you need to change details, or add something at the start to make the ending plausible or satisfying. Perhaps you'll have better ideas as you work and create a different story than the one you intended to write. You may have to research subjects to check your facts are correct, and the research may lead to the story taking a new direction. Maybe you'll end up deleting the initial prompt or idea entirely as it no longer fits in with the rest. It's possible your short story will transform into a poem, novel or article. None of that is cheating, that's writing.

Can I switch my character's gender?

Of course!

I've sometimes suggested the character be male or female, but it's fine to change that aspect. Maybe I've suggested first person (I am writing this story) but you'll prefer to use third person (Sam is writing this story) or even second (you are writing this story). That's fine too.

You may begin your story writing about a man and later decide it works better with a woman in the lead role. Or two women, or someone older or younger. You may want to remove a character, give them a different job or relationship, or change the setting or period of your story. Go for it.

In fact it's fine to change anything at any time if you feel that will result in a better piece of writing.

Did I misunderstand the prompt?

Absolutely not!

You may use these prompts in any way you wish. If you write something based on a prompt and then see the scene suggestion approaches the idea very differently, or you're doing this in a group and your piece is nothing like whatever the others have written, that does NOT mean you got it wrong.

Using a prompt or suggestion in a different way to how others have interpreted it is excellent. No editor, publisher, competition judge or reader wants a bunch of stories all very similar to each other. If you have more than one idea for any piece of writing, I'd generally urge you to ignore the first, most obvious one, and go for the storyline nobody else will be writing.

If you're inspired to write an article, poem or play instead of a story, that's great too. I want to get you writing, not dictate what you produce.

Do I really have to write every day?

Definitely not. For some that's the most productive approach, others simply can't manage that or find it suits them better to take breaks. However, I do suggest you write as regularly and frequently as you can manage and are comfortable with.

What if I don't want to start a new piece each time?

Then don't!

You can use these prompts and exercises to add to work you've already begun, start a new piece with each one, or join two or more of the exercises together to form a longer piece.

Can I submit work based on an idea in this book?

Yes – it's your story. I hope you do create something (or lots of somethings) to submit and that it's published or earns you a prize.

If you sell it for lots of money, and later bump into me outside a cake shop, I have an idea about how we could celebrate your success – but what you do with any of my ideas is always entirely up to you.

1st January

<u>Prompt</u>

Keeping resolutions

<u>Quick exercise</u>

List any resolutions you've made (New Year's or any other promises you've made to yourself) and whether you stuck to them. If you've never made any explain why.

<u>Story/scene suggestion</u>

Your character is looking back on a resolution they made and tried hard to keep. Were they successful and how do they feel about their efforts?

2nd January

<u>Prompt</u>

A risky venture

<u>Quick exercise</u>

Describe a risk, big or small, you've taken.

<u>Story/scene suggestion</u>

Your character has the choice of taking a risk with the possibility of huge rewards, or playing it safe for a much more modest outcome. How do they decide and is it the right choice?

3rd January

<u>Prompt</u>

It's all Greek to me

<u>Quick exercise</u>

List all the foreign words you can think of which are often included in works written in English. Try to use these in (English) sentences.

<u>Story/scene suggestion</u>

Your character is in conversation with people whose first language is not the same as theirs. How well do they communicate and how do they react to this challenge?

4th January

<u>Prompt</u>

Boo!

<u>Quick exercise</u>

An eerie figure appears before you. What could it do to convince you it was a ghost, or if you already believe in ghosts, how do you recognise that this is one?

<u>Story/scene suggestion</u>

Your character starts off as either strongly believing or not believing in the existence of ghosts and then experiences something which makes them doubt that position.

5th January

<u>Prompt</u>

I could read him like a book

<u>Quick exercise</u>

Describe a time when you could tell exactly how a person felt without them saying anything. What were the clues?

<u>Story/scene suggestion</u>

Your character reads the body language of another character and assumes they understand how he feels. What's the situation? Are they right?

6th January

<u>Prompt</u>

In at the deep end

<u>Quick exercise</u>

Describe swimming without using the words water, swim, swimming, swum, swam or swimmer.

<u>Story/scene suggestion</u>

Your character must explain an action to someone who has never experienced or seen it.

7th January

<u>Prompt</u>

It started well

<u>Quick exercise</u>

Read only the opening three paragraphs of a story in a magazine you'd like to be published in, or book in the genre you want to write – and then write your own version of the next three paragraphs.

<u>Story/scene suggestion</u>

Finish the whole story/chapter.

Note – if you create a whole story, you'll then also need to write a very different opening if you want to publish it, as using someone else's work without permission, even if it's just a few lines, is a breach of copyright.

Alternatively, with a friend or in a group, each write an opening scene, swap these and continue writing. You may like to agree in advance to give up copyright to your openings.

8th January

<u>Prompt</u>

Wrong end of the stick

<u>Quick exercise</u>

When did you misunderstand something that was said to you, or someone misunderstood what you said?

<u>Story/scene suggestion</u>

Your character has either misunderstood something said to them or been misunderstood themselves. He doesn't realise any misunderstanding has taken place until the misinformation has been acted on. How does he find out what happened? Is he able to sort it out – and does he choose to try?

9th January

Prompt

Home

Quick exercise

Describe your ideal home – however unrealistic or impractical it might be.

Story/scene suggestion

Your character finds their ideal home, but someone else lives there and won't give it up. Do they find a way to get them out, persuade (or force) them to share, or to accept it will never be theirs?

10th January

Prompt

Bath night

Quick exercise

What's the longest time you went without a proper wash and how did you feel about that?

Story/scene suggestion

Your character has been unable to wash for a long time. Why? How do they feel when they finally get the opportunity, and is it a shower, bath, or dip in a lake?

11th January

Prompt

The walls have ears

Quick exercise

Have you ever known, or thought, your conversation was being overheard? How did/would you react if that was the case?

Story/scene suggestion

Your character believes their conversation is being listened to. They wish to pass on information to someone whilst giving away as little as possible to whoever is listening in. What's the situation and how do they disguise or limit what they reveal?

12th January

Prompt

Never again!

Quick exercise

Describe something you've done and never want to do again.

Story/scene suggestion

A character is for some reason compelled to, or put in a situation where they must, repeat an experience which didn't go well and which they'd hoped to avoid in the future.

13th January

Prompt

Too good to be true

Quick exercise

Which minor snags, difficulties or annoyances of daily life would you most like to be able to avoid?

Story/scene suggestion

Write about a perfect character living a perfect life – no flaws snags or obstacles. Now add in a hint of conflict, have something go wrong, or introduce a minor physical or character blemish and see how they react.

14th January

Prompt

It's yours

Quick exercise

You can have any one object in the world. What would you choose and why?

Story/scene suggestion

Your character acquires the thing they thought they wanted most in the world. Does it bring the happiness they thought it would, and are they now satisfied or do they want something else?

15th January

Prompt

Responsible adult

Quick exercise

What event, behaviour or physical sign made you realise you were growing up, or had grown up?

Story/scene suggestion

Your character is forced to acknowledge they're no longer as young as they were and to consider making age appropriate changes to their life. What changes do they think of, and do they carry them through?

16th January

Prompt

Just needs the finishing touch

Quick exercise

Describe any unfinished project you've seen, and how you feel/felt about it.

Story/scene suggestion

A character discovers an almost complete piece of art or craftwork, knows the creator can't finish it and feels compelled to do it themselves. Why do they feel that way and how do they get on?

17th January

Prompt

Reading room

Quick exercise

Describe, in detail, your favourite place to read and/or write.

Story/scene suggestion

Your character has a favourite spot to read, knit, do sudoku, etc. Describe them looking forward to the chance to relax there and then it happening – or them missing the expected opportunity.

18th January

Prompt

Poor timing

Quick exercise

Describe situations you've been in where things would have turned out better if you'd arrived earlier or later, or if a specific event had happened at a different time.

Story/scene suggestion

Your character arrives for an event and either the time of their arrival, or the timing of an incident causes problems. What happens and can they overcome it?

19th January

Prompt

A stitch in time saves nine

Quick exercise

Write your memory of mending or repairing something, or attempting to do so. You might like to send that, along with a photo, as a 'tip' to one of the women's magazines which pay up to £50 for such fillers.

Story/scene suggestion

A precious possession belonging to your character is damaged. Explain how that happened, whether they choose to have it repaired, replaced, throw it out, or keep it as it is, and how they now feel about the item.

20th January

Prompt

A snow day

Quick exercise

How do you feel about snow?

Story/scene suggestion

A character experiences extreme and unexpected weather conditions.

21st January

Prompt

Copycat

Quick exercise

Has anyone ever copied you? Would you mind if they did?

Story/scene suggestion

Your character is attempting to copy someone. Why and what steps does she taken in order to accomplish this?

22nd January

Prompt

Reverse

Quick exercise

Find a poem you like and rewrite it as prose. And/or find a piece of prose you like and convert it, or part of it, into poetry.

Story/scene suggestion

Have a character speak 'poetically' in some way. Perhaps by using beautiful phrases and descriptions, maybe overuse of rhyming slang, perhaps often quoting or misquoting classic poetry.

23rd January

Prompt

Dairy free

Quick exercise

A person has opted for a limited diet or has no choice but to avoid certain foods. What foods are they excluding and why?

Story/scene suggestion

A person is excluding certain foods from their diet, but doesn't want to draw attention to this. Why does he avoid particular foods, and how successful is he in keeping his eating habits private?

24th January

Prompt

An unforgettable experience

Quick exercise

Describe an event in your life you'd like to relive.

Story/scene suggestion

A character has the opportunity to repeat any event from their past but if they do they'll then lose their memories of whatever it was. Do they accept the offer?

25th January

Prompt

So not a morning person

Quick exercise

What's your favourite time of day and why?

Story/scene suggestion

What are your character's favourite and least favourite times of day? Why? How do they make the most of one and cope with the other?

26th January

Prompt

Easy peasy

Quick exercise

Describe something you find quite easy but which you know can be more of a struggle for others.

Story/scene suggestion

Your character is naturally good at something a friend or family member is hopeless at. She can't understand why they're so unwilling to spend time doing whatever it is, or is annoyed at their failure to do it well.

27th January

Prompt

Family feeling

Quick exercise

List the people you consider to be your family. How are you different from people who would compile a much longer, or shorter, list?

Story/scene suggestion

Your character discovers there was a mistake or cover up and either they're part of a family they were unaware of, or they're not actually related to the people they thought were family.

28th January

Prompt

Dear Sir

Quick exercise

Imagine you could write a letter to a young version of any historical figure. Who would it be to and what would you say?

Story/scene suggestion

A person from the past receives a letter sent from the present day. What does it say and how do they react to the information?

29th January

Prompt

Instantly talented

Quick exercise

If you could instantly acquire a new skill, what would it be?

Story/scene suggestion

Your character can instantly gain a new skill, perhaps multiple times, but only in exchange for a skill they already possess. What do they learn and what abilities do they lose as a result?

30th January

Prompt

Pens down now

Quick exercise

Imagine you're no longer allowed to write. What would you do instead?

Story/scene suggestion

Why would someone want to stop another person writing and how could the writer continue without being found out?

31st January

Prompt

So sleepy

Quick exercise

When have you struggled to stay awake?

Story/scene suggestion

Your character is having difficulty staying awake, even though it's important that they do. What's at stake if they fall asleep and how do they try to make sure they don't?

Bonus prompt

A little light reading

Bonus exercise

Open a book and write down every third word until you have a dozen. Join these together into sentences, repeating as many as you wish, but using as few 'new' words as possible.

Bonus story/scene suggestion

Use the same dozen words, with as many extra as you like, to create a story or scene.

1st February

Prompt

Can't see the wood for the trees

Quick exercise

Describe a tree without using the words tree, leaf or wood.

Story/scene suggestion

Your character has a strong like or dislike of woodland – write a scene/story where they're walking through a forest.

2nd February

Prompt

In the beginning

Quick exercise

Which came first, the chicken or the egg? Give one possible explanation for each being true.

Story/scene suggestion

Your character is involved in a discussion where both parties hold very different opinions. Does she keep arguing until proven right, or agree to disagree?

3rd February

Prompt

Signature style

Quick exercise

Describe your usual look – clothes, hair, make-up, jewellery, etc. Why do you make some of the choices you do?

Story/scene suggestion

Your character must disguise themselves. Why? And how do they go about this?

4th February

Prompt

New kid on the block

Quick exercise

Write about a time you were the new person somewhere.

Story/scene suggestion

Your character has to completely give up almost everything familiar – location, job, friends, name. Why, and how do they cope?

5th February

Prompt

Nice weather

Quick exercise

Describe your favourite weather.

Story/scene suggestion

Your character is doing something which is weather dependent. What weather do they hope for, and what do they get?

6th February

Prompt

A rose by any other name

Quick exercise

Describe a flower without naming it, but in such detail and using any appropriate references, so that anyone reading would be able to identify it from amongst a selection of blooms.

Story/scene suggestion

Your character gives or receives flowers – the choice of colours or varieties is deeply symbolic in some way.

7th February

Prompt

Fight!

Quick exercise

Write about an argument or fight you've witnessed.

Story/scene suggestion

Your character witnesses a row or fight which is escalating in ferocity or numbers of participants or both. What do they do? Does it help or not?

8th February

Prompt

All alone

Quick exercise

When was the last time you were, or felt, alone?

Story/scene suggestion

Write about a character who is either alone from choice, or unwillingly lonely, for much of the time.

9th February

Prompt

Home sweet home

Quick exercise

Describe a room in your home – but either 100 years in the future or the past (if your home isn't that old, imagine an equivalent building of the right age). What's different, what's the same?

Story/scene suggestion

Your character is in a room which is oddly familiar, despite it being from a completely different time. Describe what she notices and why she's in a room which is, or appears to be, from another time.

10th February

Prompt

Good enough to eat

Quick exercise

If your or your character were a cake, which would it be and why?

Story/scene suggestion

Put your character in a situation where they have to create a representation of themselves in cake, or other creative format. Why are they doing this and how do they go about it?

11th February

Prompt

Love at first sight

Quick exercise

Describe your first crush in as much detail as you can remember.

Story/scene suggestion

Your character meets someone they once had a crush on, but hasn't seen lately. How do they feel now?

12th February

Prompt

Odd socks

Quick exercise

When have you gone out with odd shoes, a mis-buttoned shirt or otherwise not looking as you'd intended?

Story/scene suggestion

Your character deliberately dresses in a manner which she hopes will appear as though she's made no effort at all. Why does she do this and does it produce the result she was hoping for?

13th February

Prompt

Go on, ask me

Quick exercise

When have you ever said or done something to encourage questions or interest in your activities, or come across others doing this?

Story/scene suggestion

Your character won't just say anything straight out. It's always 'guess who I saw today'? or 'you won't believe what happened in the library'. Show how others react to this style of conversation.

14th February

Prompt

Kiss me quick

Quick exercise

How was your first kiss? (Or how do you imagine it will be?)

Story/scene suggestion

Your character has just been kissed by someone who has never kissed them before. How does this make them feel? What happens next?

15th February

Prompt

Delicious

Quick exercise

Describe, in detail, the flavour and texture of any food you enjoy without comparing it with any other food item.

Story/scene suggestion

Your character has either lost and now regained their sense of taste or has developed a sense of taste for the first time. Show them enjoying a meal.

16th February

<u>Prompt</u>

What a photograph!

<u>Quick exercise</u>

When have you taken a photograph which surprised you, or seen one that doesn't seem to have come out exactly as the photographer intended?

<u>Story/scene suggestion</u>

You character takes, or discovers, a photo that reveals something which wasn't intended to be captured on on camera.

17th February

<u>Prompt</u>

Did you hear that?

<u>Quick exercise</u>

Sit still and close your eyes. What can you hear?

<u>Story/scene suggestion</u>

Your character can hear a noise, but can't pinpoint the source. It disturbs her in some way, so she tries to locate and stop it.

18th February

<u>Prompt</u>

It's mine

<u>Quick exercise</u>

What's the first object you remember owning?

<u>Story/scene suggestion</u>

Your character has an item that has been in their possession for as long as they can remember. Now either they must give it up, or choose to do so. Why, and how do they feel?

19th February

<u>Prompt</u>

Stop me if you've heard this one

<u>Quick exercise</u>

Recount an anecdote of someone else's that you've heard several times.

<u>Story/scene suggestion</u>

Your character is repeatedly on the receiving end of a particular anecdote. What is it? Does it differ during the telling? Are they happy to keep hearing it?

20th February

<u>Prompt</u>

Dear diary

<u>Quick exercise</u>

If you don't usually keep a diary, write a summary of whatever happened yesterday. Or if that's something you regularly do, write in extreme detail about a minor event or action you wouldn't usually include.

<u>Story/scene suggestion</u>

Have your character keep a diary. How open and honest are they? Will they let anyone see it?

21st February

<u>Prompt</u>

Headline news

<u>Quick exercise</u>

Read a newspaper headline (online if necessary – but don't let the internet distract you!) and then sketch out a possible article. You can either write what you think it really says, or a piece of pure fantasy which fits the title.

<u>Story/scene suggestion</u>

Use a real news story as the basis for a piece of fiction, but change some key facts, including something which impacts on the outcome.

22nd February

Prompt

That's never happened before

Quick exercise

Describe something you've done numerous times and which has a predictable outcome.

Story/scene suggestion

You character carries out an action (or series of actions) which usually has the same result. This time something unexpected happens, or there is no result at all.

23rd February

Prompt

Friday nights

Quick exercise

What's something you do, or don't do, on a particular day of the week?

Story/scene suggestion

Your character has one or more routine behaviours associated with the day, or days, of the week. Something happens to disrupt this which has lasting repercussions. What happens and is it good or bad for the character?

24th February

Prompt

Being born

Quick exercise

Describe your earliest memory.

Story/scene suggestion

You've described your earliest memory to someone who reveals it couldn't possibly have happened they way you recall.

25th February

Prompt

The sincerest form of flattery

Quick exercise

Search online, or via writing magazines and books, for the writing techniques and tips of your favourite authors. Which are you tempted to try?

Story/scene suggestion

Your character must imitate the work or methods of another person. Why and how do they go about it?

26th February

Prompt

Initially

Quick exercise

Write as many words as you can think of which are alliterative with your name (start with the same letter). Queenie, Xavier and Zackary – you can use your surname if you prefer!

Story/scene suggestion

Your character has trouble pronouncing a particular letter – how do they limit the amount of times they're compelled to try?

27th February

Prompt

Today's the day

Quick exercise

Which is your favourite day of the year and why?

Story/scene suggestion

Write a scene or story which takes place on your character's favourite day of the year.

28th February

Prompt

Easy, Tiger!

Quick exercise

Pick someone you know, or know of, and describe them as though they were an animal.

Story/scene suggestion

Complete the above exercise with two different people (real or imaginary) and have the two individuals interact in ways which reflect their inner (or outer!) animals.

29th February

Prompt

Bonus day

Quick exercise

If you had an unexpected free day in which you could spend doing anything you liked, what would you do?

Story/scene suggestion

Your character is able to act when those around him can't. He has the opportunity to catch up on tasks, gain an advantage over rivals, help friends with chores or just have fun. What does he do?

1st March

Prompt

Not as described

Quick exercise

When was something very different from the way it was described to you?

Story/scene suggestion

A character has made a purchase and afterwards discovered what they bought differs greatly in some way from that which they'd expected. Is this a positive or negative thing and what do they do?

2nd March

Prompt

Dinner is served

Quick exercise

List the ingredients of your favourite meal. Don't limit yourself just to the food, include anything which adds to the experience.

Story/scene suggestion

Have your character make a meal which reminds them of a particular event or person.

3rd March

Prompt

Private and confidential

Quick exercise

You open a letter addressed to you from your doctor, but soon suspect the letter inside is for someone else. What does it say?

Story/scene suggestion

You receive a medical report intended for some you know, or know of, and realise the news will have a big impact on them. What do you do? What happens to this person as a result of what's in the report and your actions?

4th March

<u>Prompt</u>

Family flowers only, please

<u>Quick exercise</u>

Read an obituary of someone you don't know and imagine further details about their life based on the facts given. (Local papers and their online versions should have some.)

<u>Story/scene suggestion</u>

Your character is asked to write an obituary or give a eulogy for someone they have strong feelings about (favourable or otherwise) and wishes to hint at more than they actually say or even lie or hide information – how do they do this?

5th March

<u>Prompt</u>

Slow progress

<u>Quick exercise</u>

What's the slowest journey you've ever taken (or which felt like it at the time)?

<u>Story/scene suggestion</u>

Your character is on a real or metaphoric journey which it seems will never end. How do they feel about this and what action, if any, do they take?

6th March

<u>Prompt</u>

Naming names

<u>Quick exercise</u>

Would your life be different if you'd had a completely different name?

<u>Story/scene suggestion</u>

A character changes their name. Does it have the result they hoped?

7th March

<u>Prompt</u>

First impressions

<u>Quick exercise</u>

Think of a person you dislike and one you like and make a list of the good and bad qualities of each. (And then destroy the list about the person you dislike – or at least remove their name from the top!)

<u>Story/scene suggestion</u>

Your character meets someone and instantly dislikes them, for good reason, and then changes their mind. Why did they not like them? What changes their mind?

8th March

<u>Prompt</u>

Colourful

<u>Quick exercise</u>

As a child, what was your favourite colour and what did you have in that shade?

<u>Story/scene suggestion</u>

Your character's clothes, possessions and surroundings are of one predominant colour. What is it and why is so much in that colour?

9th March

<u>Prompt</u>

Animal behaviour

<u>Quick exercise</u>

Watch a pet or other animal and describe their behaviour or actions in a way which suggests their personality.

<u>Story/scene suggestion</u>

You encounter an animal which is acting in an unusual manner. What is it doing and why?

10th March

Prompt

Precious gem

Quick exercise

You've won a prize of a piece of personalised jewellery, handmade especially for you. What would you like?

Story/scene suggestion

Your character is given a piece of personalised, handmade jewellery, chosen by someone else. Why is she given it and what are its special features?

11th March

Prompt

First name, last name

Quick exercise

Describe someone who shares your name. What things do you have in common and what differences are there?

Story/scene suggestion

Your character is expecting to meet someone about whom they know only the name. They form opinions based on this. What are they, and are they accurate?

12th March

Prompt

I promise

Quick exercise

Explain a promise you've made to anyone other than yourself.

Story/scene suggestion

Your character made a promise, fully intending to keep it, but now either must, or chooses to, break it.

13th March

Prompt

Holding the baby

Quick exercise

Describe the first time you were left alone with someone else's baby (or elderly relative, kitten, etc. if that's never happened).

Story/scene suggestion

Your character is left alone with a helpless person or animal. They'll have the responsibility of caring for them for long enough they'll have to feed them and carry out other tasks to keep them healthy and comfortable.

14th March

Prompt

Picture perfect

Quick exercise

Either ask someone to show you a picture you've not seen before, type 'images' into Google, or open an illustrated publication at random, and describe what you see.

Story/scene suggestion

Your character is in the scene, has the object, or is looking at the picture described above. What happens next?

15th March

Prompt

#hacked

Quick exercise

You have access to a famous person's Twitter or Facebook account. Whose would you choose, and what would you be tempted to post?

Story/scene suggestion

Your character gains access to someone's social media account. What do they post and what happens next?

16th March

<u>Prompt</u>

Tied up

<u>Quick exercise</u>

Describe being physically trapped or restrained in some way.

<u>Story/scene suggestion</u>

Have your character metaphorically trapped in a situation or relationship and compare this with the feeling of being physically trapped.

17th March

<u>Prompt</u>

Sick day

<u>Quick exercise</u>

You were told a colleague was off sick, or someone avoided a social occasion claiming they were ill, but you see them somewhere soon after and they look fine. What could be going on?

<u>Story/scene suggestion</u>

You discover a colleague lied about being ill in order to take a day off work, but they did/do have a good reason not to go in. What's the real reason, and will you keep quiet to help them?

18th March

<u>Prompt</u>

Wonderful day

<u>Quick exercise</u>

Describe your ideal holiday or day out.

<u>Story/scene suggestion</u>

Your character experiences what would be your perfect day, but it's not all to their taste. What don't they like and why?

19th March

<u>Prompt</u>

Supermarket sweep

<u>Quick exercise</u>

Imagine your character doing their grocery shopping. List what they'd typically buy and any other details which occur to you.

<u>Story/scene suggestion</u>

Do your next food shop as your character. Where would he shop? What would he buy? If he generally uses a different supermarket, or shops in a very different way, how would he react to the range/prices/displays in your preferred store? Try to walk, behave and react like your character (if he's a serial killer pick his day off!)

20th March

<u>Prompt</u>

Spell it out

<u>Quick exercise</u>

Write character's full name down the page and describe them using the letters to start words e.g.

Purple

Aries

Terrific

Silly

Yodels.*

<u>Story/scene suggestion</u>

Incorporate the words created from your character's acrostic (as created in the above exercise) into a few paragraphs about your character.

*I can't really yodel.

21st March

Prompt

Let us pray

Quick exercise

Imagine you're setting up a cult or new, possibly fake, religion. What would your ten commandments be?

Story/scene suggestion

Your character encounters someone with very different beliefs from their own. How do they react to these and how do the two characters interact?

22nd March

Prompt

Seeing a pattern

Quick exercise

Make an ink blot test (put drops of any coloured liquid on a sheet of paper, fold it in half, squish it together and then open up). What do you see?

Story/scene suggestion

Your character notices the pattern formed by tea leaves, spilled milk or similar and this encourages a certain course of action.

23rd March

Prompt

When I were a lad

Quick exercise

Where were you twenty years ago? What were you doing? (If you're under twenty-five answer for when you were half the age you are now.)

Story/scene suggestion

Write a story, or flashback in a longer work, set in that time and place. Use as many real details as you can recall, but a fictional plot.

24th March

Prompt

I before E

Quick exercise

Use some words you frequently misspell in sentences – then look them up and correct any mistakes.

Story/scene suggestion

Your character spells a word incorrectly (accidentally or otherwise). This has a relatively serious, or unexpectedly good, outcome.

25th March

Prompt

Get uncomfortable

Quick exercise

Write about feeling comfortable, but do it in a physically different way from usual – standing on one leg if you usually sit, holding the pen in your teeth, with a piece of semi-transparent material over your eyes …

Story/scene suggestion

Imagine you could no longer use your current method to accomplish a routine task, but had to do it in a physically more demanding manner which took much longer. How would this impact on your life?

26th March

Prompt

Off grid

Quick exercise

The TV has broken, the internet is down and you've lost your phone. What will you miss most?

Story/scene suggestion

All communication technology has been disabled. Why has this happened and/or how do your characters cope?

27th March

<u>Prompt</u>

Destination unknown

<u>Quick exercise</u>

Open an atlas or spin a globe and select a location at random, or ask someone to choose somewhere for you (if you're relying on me then use Timbuktu). Without doing any research, write down all you know, or imagine, about that place.

<u>Story/scene suggestion</u>

Have one of your characters travel to, or have previously visited, any real location and describe it as accurately as possible but from their POV. You can research for this.

28th March

<u>Prompt</u>

Sorry, I forgot

<u>Quick exercise</u>

Explain a time you forgot to do something, which you should have done.

<u>Story/scene suggestion</u>

Your character has forgotten to do something that's very important to someone else. How does she either hide her mistake or make amends?

29th March

<u>Prompt</u>

Are you listening to me?

<u>Quick exercise</u>

Describe a situation where someone hasn't listened to you.

<u>Story/scene suggestion</u>

Your character is often ignored or not taken seriously, even by those who'd benefit from listening to her. How does she get people to take notice of what she says – or does she deal with this in a different way?

30th March

Prompt

It's my birthday!*

Quick exercise

Think ahead to your next 'big' birthday and note down any concerns and/or hopes you have. Then accidentally leave the hopes list around where friends or family will see it.

Story/scene suggestion

Your character anticipates his milestone birthday with either dread or eagerness. What does he hope for or fear? Describe the day itself – is it better or worse than he imagined, just as expected, or entirely different?

*It really is. Feel free to email cake.

31st March

Prompt

Take the day off

Quick exercise

Take a day off and do something non-writing related. If you wish, find another way to record or remind yourself of the experience.

Story/scene suggestion

Really do take a day off from writing. If you don't want today to be that day, write about a person forced to take a day's absence from a job they love, but make sure you take another day off sometime soon.

1st April

Prompt

Fools!

Quick exercise

Explain a practical joke or prank you've played, or which has been played on you or someone you know.

Story/scene suggestion

A character has a joke played on them and retaliates, as does the victim. How far does this go, and how is it resolved (if it is)?

2nd April

Prompt

From little acorns

Quick exercise

Describe planting a seed and watching it grow. If you've never done this you're really missing out. Buy some cress and sprout it on a windowsill and write about doing that.

Story/scene suggestion

You sow seeds, but get something very different from whatever you'd expected to grow.

3rd April

Prompt

I am me

Quick exercise

How can you prove you're really you?

Story/scene suggestion

There's a doppelgänger of your character. They must prove they're not this person. Why do they need to do this and how do they go about it?

4th April

Prompt

Crying

Quick exercise

Describe something which made you cry (happy tears are allowed).

Story/scene suggestion

Attempt to write a scene so full of emotion that it's hard to see through your own tears.

5th April

Prompt

Litter bug

Quick exercise

Someone drops litter in front of you. What is it? How do you feel/act?

Story/scene suggestion

Your character challenges someone for dropping litter. He discovers that what they dropped isn't what he thought and they had a very good reason to drop it. What is the item and why did they drop it?

6th April

Prompt

A job for life

Quick exercise

What did you want to be when you grew up? (Or if you've sensibly not grown up, what do you hope to do, should that ever happen?)

Story/scene suggestion

Your character has been brought up with the expectation of doing a particular job, or fulfilling a particular role. As an adult, they either don't wish to do this, or do but something prevents it. What happens next?

7th April

Prompt

Lots of love

Quick exercise

Describe someone (or a pet) you love in a non romantic way.

Story/scene suggestion

Your character cares very deeply for someone other than a romantic partner. What is the relationship? How does she show her feelings and how does the other person respond?

8th April

Prompt

Thank you so much

Quick exercise

What things are you grateful for?

Story/scene suggestion

Write about a character who learns to be grateful for what he has.

9th April

Prompt

Bestseller

Quick exercise

Imagine you've written a hugely successful book. Give it a title, visualise the cover, decide the genre, write the blurb (bit on the back to entice potential readers). What are people saying about it? Who is reading it? How do people react when they discover you're the author?

Story/scene suggestion

Now write that book! If you're struggling to get started, begin by expanding the blurb and/or look at the cover description you've just written and list everything the image suggests to you.

10th April

Prompt

Nice to meet you at last

Quick exercise

Describe your first physical meeting with a person you'd previously heard about, or communicated with online, by phone, etc.

Story/scene suggestion

Your character has been waiting to meet someone for a long time. It's almost happened several times but something prevented each meeting. Now they're just the other side of that door ...

11th April

Prompt

Not fair!

Quick exercise

When have you ever cheated or been the victim of a cheat?

Story/scene suggestion

Your character is betrayed by someone they thought they could rely on. How do they feel and what do they do in response?

12th April

Prompt

Imitation

Quick exercise

Copy out a section of something written by a writer you particularly admire and as you do so, note things such as sentence length, punctuation use, word choices e.g. short, complex, common, foreign, use of similes or other devices. (Include the author's name so you don't later mistakenly think it's your own work.)

Story/scene suggestion

Write, or rewrite, something of your own mirroring those aspects as closely as possible.

13th April

Prompt

Whichever you prefer

Quick exercise

Explain an occasion in which you've been unable to decide between one or more options.

Story/scene suggestion

Your character is asked their preference about a course of action, but doesn't wish to make, or declare, a preference. How does he attempt to avoid this?

14th April

Prompt

No entry

Quick exercise

Find or imagine a locked door and describe (or guess) what's behind it.

Story/scene suggestion

Your character has a job which regularly requires her to open or break down doors and she must assess the likely risks behind it first.

15th April

Prompt

Not all bad

Quick exercise

Think of a real person you know and don't particularly like and list as many positive things about them as you can. You can guess some if you don't know, but don't give them qualities you know they don't posses.

Story/scene suggestion

Your character strongly dislikes someone personally, but must write a report on them or answer questions about them and doesn't want this dislike to show. Why is that? How honest will they be?

16th April

Prompt

It's the thought that counts

Quick exercise

Describe receiving a gift you didn't like, and how you reacted.

Story/scene suggestion

Your character is given a gift that isn't just disappointing but apparently reveals something unsettling about the giver, or their opinion of the recipient. How does she react?

17th April

Prompt

Gone but not forgotten

Quick exercise

Describe an item you once treasured but no longer have.

Story/scene suggestion

Your character is reunited with a long lost treasured item.

18th April

Prompt

God bless you

Quick exercise

When has it been assumed or suggested that you hold feelings or beliefs which you don't?

Story/scene suggestion

Your character makes assumptions about the feelings or beliefs of someone else, later learning their mistake. What did they get wrong and how much did it matter?

19th April

Prompt

Down and out

Quick exercise

Describe a homeless person as negatively and unsympathetically as possible (not your opinion, but what someone with extreme views might say/think). It can just be a list of words or phrases, but include a physical description, behaviour and guess the reason for them being in this situation. Repeat, this time being as positive and sympathetic as possible.

Story/scene suggestion

Two people, each holding the above opposing views, meet and interact with the homeless person. Were any of their assumptions correct? Do either of them change their opinion? Does any of that impact for good or ill on the homeless person?

20th April

Prompt

Quick sketch

Quick exercise

Doodle on the page and describe what you've drawn.

Story/scene suggestion

Have your character unconsciously draw a doodle or idly write something random, which later becomes important.

21st April

Prompt

Away with the fairies

Quick exercise

Describe a fairy/faerie.

Story/scene suggestion

A fairy/faerie lands by your character. Describe their reactions, whether they believe it's real, and what they do next.

22nd April

Prompt

Bluff it out

Quick exercise

Look for reports on, or discussions of, a subject you know very little about (football, wine tasting, ballet dancing) and note some key phrases which crop up quite often.

Story/scene suggestion

Your character is trying to convince someone they have far greater knowledge of something than is really the case. How do they go about it. Do they get away with it?

23rd April

Prompt

Is this what I think it is?

Quick exercise

When have you thought you'd seen/heard/felt something and then realised it was something different?

Story/scene suggestion

Your character believes she sees/hears/feels something and behaves accordingly until she realises her mistake. What is the true explanation and how does she feel when she makes the discovery?

24th April

Prompt

Uniform look

Quick exercise

You can only wear the exact same clothes for the rest of your life (several sets, so you can be clean and tidy if you choose). What would you pick?

Story/scene suggestion

Your character decides to always wear identical, or similar clothing. What do they select and why are they doing this?

25th April

Prompt

Bucket list

Quick exercise

What have you long wanted to do, but not yet got around to attempting?

Story/scene suggestion

Your character has a long held ambition. Eventually they have the opportunity to fulfil it. Do they still want to? Do they go ahead with it? How do they feel after doing, or not doing, whatever it is?

26th April

Prompt

Blind date

Quick exercise

Your friend is trying to fix you up with someone. You're not interested. What would you do to put the potential date off?

Story/scene suggestion

Your character has taken steps to discourage someone who was attracted to her. She now regrets her actions. Why is she sorry she behaved as she did and what, if anything, does she do to remedy the situation?

27th April

Prompt

Who said that?

Quick exercise

Imagine you're temporarily invisible. What would you do?

Story/scene suggestion

Your character is invisible, or undetected for some other reason, and in a position to be able to do something she'd previously fantasised about doing. What is it and does she do it?

28th April

Prompt

Queue jumper

Quick exercise

Someone pushes in front of you in a queue. How do you feel?

Story/scene suggestion

You're not the sort to queue jump, but today you have to. Why and what happens?

29th April

Prompt

It's all gone dark

Quick exercise

Close your eyes and walk around the room or an open space (not a cliff edge, please!) How hard was it? Did you notice or experience anything you weren't expecting?

Story/scene suggestion

A character who'd been unable to see suddenly has sight. How do they react?

30th April

Prompt

Mr Popular

Quick exercise

Describe a person (real or imaginary) you think most people would like.

Story/scene suggestion

Your character dislikes someone who everyone else apparently considers wonderful. He decides to learn everything he can about this person. Does he uncover a less pleasant side to the individual, or come to appreciate their good qualities?

1st May

Prompt

In the beginning

Quick exercise

List any ways the world is said to have been created. Include whatever you believe to be true and things you're certain aren't right.

Story/scene suggestion

Pen your own creation story. It could be for Earth, our entire universe, or a world from your imagination.

2nd May

Prompt

Top tip

Quick exercise

List things which you wish everyone knew, but which apparently aren't common knowledge.

Story/scene suggestion

Your character discovers something they find extremely interesting, or very useful, and then realises most other people already knew.

3rd May

Prompt

Where am I?

Quick exercise

You've woken up somewhere you don't recognise. What's happened?

Story/scene suggestion

You wake up somewhere you don't recognise and with no recent memories. Gradually you realise someone is very anxious to find out exactly what you remember and you're not sure this is entirely for your benefit. What do you do as hazy memories begin to return?

4th May

Prompt

Dust

Quick exercise

Which household chore or other routine task would you give up if you could?

Story/scene suggestion

Your character suddenly stops doing something that was previously a frequent and, he'd thought, important task. What does he give up and what's the result?

5th May

Prompt

Lucky pants

Quick exercise

Describe a current, or former, favourite item of clothing.

Story/scene suggestion

Your character has a favourite item of clothing, or accessory. What is it and why is it so special to them?

6th May

Prompt

How are you?

Quick exercise

Imagine asking several different people how they are. What type of response are you likely to get?

Story/scene suggestion

Your character never gives the expected quick response to common conversational expressions such as 'how are you?' or 'have a good day' but always replies at length. Show him chatting to people and how they react over time.

7th May

Prompt

To whom it may concern

Quick exercise

You keep getting what look like birthday and christmas cards, which are addressed to someone you don't know. What do you do with them?

Story/scene suggestion

Your character receives cards addressed to someone else and opens one. Immediately they realise it's not quite the innocently misaddressed mail it originally appeared to be. What's odd about it and now what do they do?

8th May

Prompt

Run for it

Quick exercise

Describe the last time you ran.

Story/scene suggestion

Your character must run to to get help for a loved one. It's further than he's ever managed to run before and/or he must do it more quickly than he'd usually be capable of – but not so much further or faster that he feels it's impossible.

9th May

Prompt

Natural talent

Quick exercise

Which skill or attribute are you most proud of possessing and why?

Story/scene suggestion

Your character admires a particular trait or ability in someone and tries to acquire it. What does she do towards this and what's the result?

10th May

Prompt

Seeing ahead

Quick exercise

If you could look into the future and see the answers to three questions, what would they be?

Story/scene suggestion

Your character believes he's seen the future and he's not happy about what lies ahead. What actions does he take in the hope of making things happen differently and is he successful?

11th May

Prompt

It's been a while

Quick exercise

Describe someone you knew in your childhood, but haven't seen since.

Story/scene suggestion

Imagine meeting someone you've not seen since your childhood. How would you recognise each other? How much different will you seem to them? What would you tell them about the intervening period and what might they say to you?

12th May

Prompt

Don't tell a soul

Quick exercise

Recall a secret you've either revealed or uncovered.

Story/scene suggestion

Your character has promised to keep a secret, but either tells others almost immediately, or drops hints so they can guess.

13th May

Prompt

Our Lady of Fatima

Quick exercise

Today is the saint day of Our Lady of Fatima. Look her up and write a short biography for her. (Or if you're doing this on a different date, pick the appropriate saint of the day.)

Story/scene suggestion

Write a modern day version of whatever any saint was canonised for, including modern day reactions to whatever they did.

14th May

Prompt

Free sample

Quick exercise

What's the last thing you got for nothing?

Story/scene suggestion

Your character gets something apparently for nothing, but too late realises there's a catch or a price to pay.

15th May

Prompt

Alibi

Quick exercise

You're wrongly accused of a horrible crime exactly a year ago today. How do you find out, and then prove, where you really were and what you did?

Story/scene suggestion

Your character is wrongly accused of a crime which happened at least a year previously. He can't remember what he was doing and feels compelled to make something up. What does he say? What happens next?

16th May

Prompt

My mistake

Quick exercise

When have you misjudged someone or their motives, or made an unfounded assumption?

Story/scene suggestion

Your character is prejudiced against a group of people, but then has to spend time with one of them and comes to see that he was wrong, at least in this individual case.

17th May

Prompt

Colour coded

Quick exercise

Write about your day, using different coloured pens or changing the font colour as you go. Try to match words to the colours in some way.

Story/scene suggestion

Your character is especially aware of and sensitive to colour. Different shades can greatly influence their mood and behaviour.

18th May

Prompt

Cutting a long story short

Quick exercise

Explain the entire plot of the last book you read in fewer than 50 words.

Story/scene suggestion

Write a brief synopsis (plot outline) of any story of yours you've not yet finished, perhaps one you've not even started, but would like to write. This should include the ending and all major incidents. Use this to help you actually finish (it's OK to make changes if you think up better ideas later on).

19th May

Prompt

No big deal

Quick exercise

What's the best or worst that could happen if you missed the bus/train/plane?

Story/scene suggestion

Your character just misses catching a bus/train or is slightly late for an appointment. At first that seems to be only a minor problem, but they come to realise it mattered much more than they could have anticipated.

20th May

Prompt

Betrayed

Quick exercise

You discover a friend or family member you thought you could trust has lied to you. How do you feel?

Story/scene suggestion

You know someone trusts you, but you're going to lie to them. What do you say and why?

21st May

Prompt

Looks like mine

Quick exercise

You get home, put your hand in your jacket pocket/bag for your door key and realise it's not really your jacket/bag. What would you do?

Story/scene suggestion

Your character realises they've picked up someone else's bag thinking it was theirs, and that they've had it some time. What interesting things does she find in the other bag, and what is happening to her own stuff?

22nd May

Prompt

Mirror image

Quick exercise

Try writing in reverse – so it can be read the right way in a mirror (you can use the mirror to do this if it helps). The words you write should give a possible use of, or reason for, writing this way.

Story/scene suggestion

Your character speaks to someone, who interprets their words as meaning the exact opposite of the way they were intended.

23rd May

Prompt

See you later

Quick exercise

You're going to be separated from a loved one for a long period. What would you say to them?

Story/scene suggestion

Your character thought he would never see a certain person again, but is unexpectedly reunited with them after a fairly short period. How do they both react?

24th May

Prompt

Who took that?

Quick exercise

Have you ever had something stolen or deliberately hidden from you?

Story/scene suggestion

Your character realises she's lost something and has reason to suspect another character is responsible. Does she accuse them, or try to investigate? Does she learn the truth or get the item back?

25th May

Prompt

She has your eyes

Quick exercise

Find a photo of anyone but yourself. Study yourself in the mirror and list five differences and five similarities.

Story/scene suggestion

Your character is shocked to notice either striking differences or similarities between her appearance and that of someone else. What does she notice and why does it matter?

26th May

Prompt

Sport's day

Quick exercise

Explain the rules of a game or sport you enjoy, as though to someone who has never heard of it.

Story/scene suggestion

Invent, or adapt, a game or sport and have your characters play it.

27th May

Prompt

What I meant was …

Quick exercise

When have you said or written one thing but meant, or thought, something else?

Story/scene suggestion

Your character always says what he thinks people want to hear, even though it's often the opposite of what he thinks, or knows to be true. They're aware it's often irritating or can lead to trouble for themselves or others, but can't help doing it.

28th May

Prompt

Silver lining

Quick exercise

Recall complaints you've had to listen to, or find such posts on social media, and think of possible positives to the situations.

Story/scene suggestion

Write a character who always responds positively and looks on the bright side, even when such behaviour is totally inappropriate?

29th May

Prompt

As everyone knows

Quick exercise

Make one statement you think everyone will agree with and one everyone will disagree with. If possible, ask others if they do agree and disagree as expected.

Story/scene suggestion

Your character has said something they believed everyone present would agree with and discovers that's very far from the case. Why did they want agreement and what happens now they don't have it

30th May

Prompt

Adrenaline rush

Quick exercise

Describe an activity you enjoy and find exciting/exhilarating. (Yes, you can write about *that* if you wish.)

Story/scene suggestion

A character explains an activity she enjoys to someone else, but chooses her words carefully as she's trying to put the other person off having a go.

31st May

Prompt

It's raining cats and dogs

Quick exercise

List as many metaphors that you can think of. (Metaphors are figures of speech in which an action or object is described in a way which isn't literally true, but as though that were the case. There's no 'like' or 'as'.)

Story/scene suggestion

Chances are many of the metaphors which come to mind are unoriginal and clichéd. Rewrite some of them using new comparisons and then work at least one of these into a piece of your writing.

Bonus Prompt

Space to fill

Bonus exercise

Link one of these lists of words together into sentences, using as few other words as possible –

Purple, cake, envelope, slowly, wind and Saturday.

Wasp, yell, caught, shoe, laugh and tumble.

Sagittarius, iridescent, waterproof, ample and stuffing.

Colour, money, apostrophe, unlikely and hill.

Tumble, incident, tissue, glass, note and watch.

Bonus story/scene suggestion

Include all the words from one, or more, of the above groups of words in a short story or poem.

1st June

<u>Prompt</u>

Nobody gets hurt

<u>Quick exercise</u>

Do you think there is such a thing as victimless crime? Give examples if so, or state your reason for disagreeing.

<u>Story/scene suggestion</u>

Your character does something (not necessarily a crime) that she knows or feels is wrong, but which she believes won't really do anyone any harm. Later she discovers it did have negative consequences for someone. What, if anything, does she do to make amends?

2nd June

<u>Prompt</u>

Dream come true

<u>Quick exercise</u>

Write down one of your dreams (the story your brain shows you when you're asleep, not a hope or aspiration).

<u>Story/scene suggestion</u>

Either your character's dream becomes real or he gets stuck dreaming it.

3rd June

<u>Prompt</u>

Headline news

<u>Quick exercise</u>

Watch coverage of an ongoing news item and summarise the situation as simply as possible – as though to a child.

<u>Story/scene suggestion</u>

Your character has been out of communication for several months. What does she learn after catching up on world events?

4th June

Prompt

Only kidding

Quick exercise

When have you made a joke which was misinterpreted or backfired?

Story/scene suggestion

Your character overhears something shocking or surprising. He's sure it's not true and probably began as an innocent or jokey comment of his which was misinterpreted and/or exaggerated. If the rumour continues to spread and be believed it will have a serious impact on a person's life. What does he do?

5th June

Prompt

Seeing red

Quick exercise

Describe losing your temper.

Story/scene suggestion

Your character is angry and takes action to cool her temper. What annoyed her and how does she calm herself down?

6th June

Prompt

Look up

Quick exercise

Look at the clouds (or tea leaves, or coffee rings if no clouds are visible). What do you see?

Story/scene suggestion

What does your character see when she looks at the clouds? She, or another character she interacts with, expresses the belief that the clouds send messages and deduces that something specific is going to happen.

7th June

<u>Prompt</u>

Yikes!

<u>Quick exercise</u>

Write about a fear or phobia of your own, or which is experienced by someone close.

<u>Story/scene suggestion</u>

Give a character a fear or phobia and force them to face it. Do they cope? How does the experience change them?

8th June

<u>Prompt</u>

Wrong number

<u>Quick exercise</u>

Imagine getting a series of wrong number calls. How might the conversations go?

<u>Story/scene suggestion</u>

Someone makes a call to the wrong number, but they are too excited/upset/confused to realise they haven't reached the person they intended. They ask for help or want to talk. What do they, or the person they've called, do?

9th June

<u>Prompt</u>

Hair raising

<u>Quick exercise</u>

Describe your most dramatic hair cut (tattoo, makeover, etc.). How did you feel whilst it was being done and when you saw the result?

<u>Story/scene suggestion</u>

Your character has requested a very dramatic new look, but begins to wonder if the person doing it fully understood what they wanted. There are no mirrors to show what's happening and other customers and staff are starting to stare ...

10th June

Prompt

Seasonal adjustment

Quick exercise

How do you feel about each season – spring, summer autumn and winter?

Story/scene suggestion

Your character particularly likes or dislikes one season, or annual event (their birthday, Christmas, etc.) and does all they can to extend or reduce it.

11th June

Prompt

Money isn't everything

Quick exercise

List as many potential advantages as you can think of for not being extremely wealthy.

Story/scene suggestion

Your character has a sudden and extreme change in their financial situation – they may get much richer or poorer. Once over the initial shock, what unexpected advantages or disadvantages does he notice?

12th June

Prompt

DNA

Quick exercise

List places you've left DNA/fingerprints – especially places you've not been recently, but which may still hold the evidence you were once there.

Story/scene suggestion

Your character's DNA or fingerprints are found at a crime scene. She's unable to give an innocent and plausible sounding explanation for this.

13th June

Prompt

Get yourself gone

Quick exercise

If you could make one person cease to exist, or be moved so far away from you that you were no longer aware of them, who would it be and why?

Story/scene suggestion

Your character can not only make people vanish, but it's as though they'd never existed. They do this to someone they feel the world would be better without. Does this solve a problem? Are there unintended consequences?

14th June

Prompt

Message from the past

Quick exercise

Think up ways we can 'hear' from people from the past or learn from them.

Story/scene suggestion

Your character receives a message from a dead relative (perhaps many generations back). She believes it to be genuine and that others would benefit from the information so attempts to pass it on.

15th June

Prompt

Nobody's perfect

Quick exercise

List some of your flaws or weaknesses.

Story/scene suggestion

Give one of your own flaws or weaknesses to a character, but turn it into a positive.

16th June

Prompt

A lesson learned

Quick exercise

Recount something you've learned, other than as part of a standard school lesson, which has been of benefit to you.

Story/scene suggestion

Your character is a trainer or other person of influence. Later someone finds him to tell say how what they learned has impacted on their life.

17th June

Prompt

Puzzling it out

Quick exercise

List different kinds of puzzle and the type of people you know/think enjoy them.

Story/scene suggestion

Your character has recently taken up some kind of puzzling game or activity and become rather obsessed. How do they engineer opportunities to enjoy their new pastime and how does working on the puzzles impact on their daily life?

18th June

Prompt

Excuse me

Quick exercise

Write a list of excuses or reasons for not writing.

Story/scene suggestion

Have your character keep making excuses, but finally have to do whatever he was avoiding.

19th June

Prompt

Never a borrower or a lender be

Quick exercise

What things have you ever borrowed or lent out and why?

Story/scene suggestion

Your character has borrowed something, which was lent only with reluctance, and is now unable to return it. What's gone wrong and how does she deal with the situation?

20th June

Prompt

Absolutely ravenous

Quick exercise

What does it feel like to be really hungry?

Story/scene suggestion

A character's often very hungry. Does his situation deteriorate or improve?

21st June

Prompt

Touch wood

Quick exercise

Are there any superstitions you act upon (even if you don't actually believe in them)?

Story/scene suggestion

Your character is very superstitious and always does things he considers good luck and avoids anything he fears might be unlucky. What happens when he can't carry out one of these lucky rituals, or has no option to do something that's supposedly bad luck?

22nd June

Prompt

Nice hat

Quick exercise

List all the types of headgear you can think of.

Story/scene suggestion

You spot a quirky hat in a charity shop and buy it on impulse. Something odd happens when you put it on.

23rd June

Prompt

Mind the gap

Quick exercise

List reasons for pauses in conversations.

Story/scene suggestion

Your character is unable to remain silent in the presence of others.

24th June

Prompt

You deserve better

Quick exercise

Think of someone who deserves better luck or a joyful experience. What would you bring to their life if you could?

Story/scene suggestion

Your character wishes something good to happen to a deserving person. To his surprise it really happens. He is apparently able to repeat this, although it doesn't always work.

25th June

Prompt

Six of the best

Quick exercise

List your six favourite words.

Story/scene suggestion

Work your six favourite words into one piece of writing.

26th June

Prompt

Unbelievable

Quick exercise

Describe a weird coincidence or something else you'd have found difficult to believe if you hadn't seen or experienced it yourself.

Story/scene suggestion

Create a situation which makes a seemingly unlikely event perfectly plausible and believable (bring in elements of any genre you wish).

27th June

Prompt

This day in history

Quick exercise

Look up historical events which happened on today's date and write a sensationalist news headline for the event/events which interest you.

Story/scene suggestion

Write a fictionalised version of one of a historical event which occurred on today's date, or use it as a background for a different story.

28th June

Prompt

Leading the witness

Quick exercise

When have you ever misled someone, deliberately or accidentally?

Story/scene suggestion

Your character either makes an innocent remark which is misinterpreted, or deliberately says something misleading and this has a series of implications.

29th June

Prompt

Boys will be boys

Quick exercise

List ways you are typical of your nationality, race, gender or age.

Story/scene suggestion

Write a character who is untypical for their nationality, race, gender or age, yet still believable.

30th June

Prompt

At first sight

Quick exercise

Think of a person you liked on sight or at your first interaction with them. Try to work out what made you form an instantly favourable opinion.

Story/scene suggestion

Have your character form a strong and immediate liking or dislike for a person. Show why, and whether she retained this opinion after getting to know more about the person.

1st July

Prompt

The greatest gift

Quick exercise

What's the best present you ever gave someone?

Story/scene suggestion

Your character wants to give the best gift ever. Why does it matter so much, what do they give and who to?

2nd July

Prompt

Special delivery

Quick exercise

A big padded envelope has arrived, addressed to you. What's in it?

Story/scene suggestion

Your character receives an unexpected package. Something prevents them opening it immediately and they spend time speculating about what it might contain. Are they right?

3rd July

Prompt

It's raining money

Quick exercise

You find a wad of banknotes. What would you do with it?

Story/scene suggestion

Your character finds money which they start to spend. After they've disposed of more than they can quickly and easily replace, they learn something about the rightful owner which makes them regret their actions.

4th July

Prompt

Liar!

Quick exercise

Create five complete lies about yourself.

Story/scene suggestion

Someone has been lying about your character. What did they say, why, and what does your character do?

5th July

Prompt

Get packing

Quick exercise

A friend rings saying they've got a spare ticket for a wonderful trip, they'll be outside your house in six minutes and you can come if you're packed and ready. What items would you grab to take?

Story/scene suggestion

Your character must pack for a trip in a very short time and/or take only a small bag. What do they take? Why?

6th July

Prompt

The blonde

Quick exercise

List people you know, or know of, who can be described using one dominant physical attribute.

Story/scene suggestion

Your character is physically distinctive in some way. What's their noticeable feature and do they find it an advantage or disadvantage?

7th July

Prompt

Hoax

Quick exercise

Find a hoax (anything which instructs people to 'copy and paste, don't share' on Facebook is a likely source) and write how you feel about it, or how you'd feel if you or someone else fell for it.

Story/scene suggestion

Write from the viewpoint of someone creating a hoax. Why do they do it? What happens to them?

8th July

Prompt

Mrs Average

Quick exercise

Describe the most normal person you can think of.

Story/scene suggestion

Put a normal person in a situation where they stand out as unusual.

9th July

Prompt

Blush

Quick exercise

Confess to something embarrassing. You can delete the details of whatever is was as soon as you've finished, but keep notes on how you felt.

Story/scene suggestion

Your character did something extremely embarrassing, which will cause them trouble if it's made public. They, or a friend, are now accused of a crime and the only way to prove them not guilty is to confess to what really happened.

10th July

Prompt

Silence please

Quick exercise

Without the sound on, watch a short burst of a TV programme you don't usually see. Write down what you think just happened.

Story/scene suggestion

Your character sees, or hears, something happen, but not both. He describes it later, without mentioning he only got half the story and guessed the rest. He got some details wrong – does that matter?

11th July

Prompt

Are you sitting comfortably?

Quick exercise

Lots of writers have 'rituals' or habits to get them in the right frame of mind to write. List anything which would make you feel comfortable when starting to write, or which you can do to avoid distractions once you've got going. Try to get in the habit of doing these before each writing session.

Story/scene suggestion

Your character develops a ritual before doing a certain task or action. What do they do, and what's it in preparation for?

12th July

Prompt

The day job

Quick exercise

List as many jobs as you can.

Story/scene suggestion

Your character has had an enormous number of different jobs. He's now attempting to get a new one.

13th July

<u>Prompt</u>

Say cheese

<u>Quick exercise</u>

List things which make you smile.

<u>Story/scene suggestion</u>

Your character wants people to smile at him. Why? How does he try to make this happen? Does it work?

14th July

<u>Prompt</u>

Ten years from now

<u>Quick exercise</u>

What changes do you think will have happened to you and your life in ten year's time?

<u>Story/scene suggestion</u>

Your character either travels ten years into the future, or has been in a coma, suffers memory loss, been away somewhere remote, etc. so it appears that way to them.

15th July

<u>Prompt</u>

That's handy

<u>Quick exercise</u>

Describe all the types of glove you can think of.

<u>Story/scene suggestion</u>

It's very important that your character wears gloves for a period of time. Why? What will happen if they lose one?

16th July

<u>Prompt</u>

Finders keepers

<u>Quick exercise</u>

Explain the circumstances behind you, accidentally or deliberately, taking something which wasn't yours.

<u>Story/scene suggestion</u>

Your character has taken something that isn't his, or he wasn't entitled to, but doesn't realise this until later. It's something he'd like to keep. What does he do?

17th July

<u>Prompt</u>

Lost

<u>Quick exercise</u>

Describe what happened and how you felt when you got lost.

<u>Story/scene suggestion</u>

Write one piece from the point of view of a person who has got lost, gone missing or run away and another using the viewpoint of someone who notices their absence and decides whether or not to search for them.

18th July

<u>Prompt</u>

Lower Upham

<u>Quick exercise</u>

Find interesting place names and imagine the people who might live there.

<u>Story/scene suggestion</u>

Your character's address or place of birth is so unusual that whenever she has to provide this information she meets with disbelief or amusement.

19th July

Prompt

A load of rubbish

Quick exercise

What's usually in your rubbish bin and what does that reveal about you?

Story/scene suggestion

Reveal your character's personality by describing what they throw out.

20th July

Prompt

Storm in a teacup

Quick exercise

Write about someone making a cup of tea in such a way that it shows they're experiencing a great deal of emotion.

Story/scene suggestion

Have your character repeat a routine action, such as making a cup of tea, several times. On each occasion they're experiencing a different emotion.

21st July

Prompt

Everyone's a critic

Quick exercise

Write a review (perhaps on Amazon or Goodreads,) of the last book you read*, saying what you particular liked and/or disliked about it. Do this regularly and try to avoid everything you dislike, and include some things you do like, in your own writing.

Story/scene suggestion

Your character rights a hilarious (intentionally or otherwise) review of a product which is shared all over social media and mentioned on a TV programme. He's contacted directly by the creator of the product.

*Do it for this one when you've finished and I'll be *very* grateful.

22nd July

Prompt

Distant past

Quick exercise

Describe a place you knew in your childhood but haven't been to since.

Story/scene suggestion

Your character returns to a location they'd not expected to visit again.

23rd July

Prompt

What happened was …

Quick exercise

Rewrite an experience you've been told about as though it happened to you.

Story/scene suggestion

Your character often mentions things which have happened to others as though he himself were directly involved. Why does he do this, and does anyone realise he's lying?

24th July

Prompt

Our tune

Quick exercise

List your favourite songs

Story/scene suggestion

Write a story based on the lyrics of one of your favourite songs. (It's OK to use the same basic idea in your own story, but you can't include the actual lyrics if you hope to publish the story.)

25th July

Prompt

How rude!

Quick exercise

Give example of ways people can be rude.

Story/scene suggestion

Have your character be unintentionally rude. Why didn't they realise what they'd done or said would be considered rude? How does the person they were rude to feel or act?

26th July

Prompt

Excuse me, aren't you …?

Quick exercise

You meet a famous person in a lift and they agree to answer three questions. Who would you like to meet? What would you ask?

Story/scene suggestion

Your character is often mistaken for someone famous. What do they get asked and how do they respond?

27th July

Prompt

Oi!

Quick exercise

When has someone called out at you?

Story/scene suggestion

Someone calls out to your character. It's not an unusual occurrence, but this time she can't make out what is being said. Does she ignore it, or try to find out what was said? How does the incident impact on what happens to them later?

28th July

Prompt

I can't stop

Quick exercise

Describe a chaotic, or out of control, moment or event in your life.

Story/scene suggestion

Put your character in a situation which gradually spirals out of their control.

29th July

Prompt

First class post

Quick exercise

Write a letter of praise or admiration to a real person or organisation. Post it to them.

Story/scene suggestion

Your character writes fan mail or a letter of thanks to someone, not expecting to get a reply, but they do, and it's definitely not just an automatic, standard response.

30th July

Prompt

The long and short of it

Quick exercise

You must choose between being much shorter or taller than you currently are. Which would you chose and why?

Story/scene suggestion

Your character either grows or shrinks to a noticeable extent. How does this change their life?

31st July

Prompt

Cause for concern

Quick exercise

Write about a cause you care deeply about.

Story/scene suggestion

Write about a character who doesn't care about something, but begins to after an incident forces them to take notice.

Bonus prompt

Totally at random

Bonus exercise

Try to quickly write twenty random words completely unconnected to each other. Don't stop to think, just write.

Bonus story/scene suggestion

Link some of the random words listed above together, so they form a short story or scene.

If in a group, ask each person to pick one or two words for everyone to link together independently. You can also find online Scrabble or word association games and use the last few entries.

1st August
Prompt
Hocus pocus
Quick exercise
If you could make a magic potion or cast a spell, what would it do?
Story/scene suggestion
Your character has, believes they have, the ability to do some kind of magic. How do they use, or try to use, this power?

2nd August
Prompt
Lost and found
Quick exercise
Imagine you've lost something and must describe it in detail, or prove ownership, so the person finding it is convinced it's really yours.
Story/scene suggestion
A character loses something that he's happy to have seen the last of, but feels obliged to report its loss or be seen to be trying to recover it. Why does he feel that way, what actions does he take, and what's the outcome?

3rd August
Prompt
Herbal remedies
Quick exercise
Give your thoughts on alternative medicines and treatments (crystals, healing hands, aromatherapy, etc.).
Story/scene suggestion
Your character has a medical problem and, although sceptical, is persuaded to try an alternative therapy of some kind. His symptoms clear up.

4th August

Prompt

Thanks for writing

Quick exercise

List as many times as you can think of when your writing has pleased someone (even if it's just your signature on a cheque).

Story/scene suggestion

Write about your character's written or spoken words bringing joy to an individual or to many people.

5th August

Prompt

Woman's interest

Quick exercise

List hobbies and interests generally associated quite strongly with either men or women.

Story/scene suggestion

Your character is involved in a group activity where most of the other people are of the opposite gender. How well do they fit in? What challenges do they face?

6th August

Prompt

Apricity

Quick exercise

Open the dictionary, find a word you didn't know and incorporate it into a sentence.

Story/scene suggestion

Complete the above exercise twice more, then connect the sentences, adding as many extra words (or paragraphs!) as you need for it to make some kind of sense.

7th August

Prompt

Romance in the air

Quick exercise

What's the most romantic situation you've ever been in?

Story/scene suggestion

Your character witnesses a romantic or touching scene. How do they feel about it?

8th August

Prompt

First time for everything

Quick exercise

Write your memories of doing something for the first time.

Story/scene suggestion

Think of something you've never done, then have your character do, or prepare to do it. You can research this, or write from your imagination – but if you intend to publish or submit it you should check you've got the facts right first.

9th August

Prompt

Twenty-two

Quick exercise

What's your favourite/lucky number and why?

Story/scene suggestion

Your character has strong connections with a certain number, feels it's symbolic or very lucky or unlucky. What happens when this number crops up in their life?

10th August

Prompt

The last time

Quick exercise

Describe something you've done for what's likely to be the last time.

Story/scene suggestion

Your character is just about to do something for the very last time. Is she saddened or relieved?

11th August

Prompt

Nailed it!

Quick exercise

Describe something you struggled to master and how you felt when you finally got it right.

Story/scene suggestion

Have your character want to do, or learn, something that it seems unlikely he'll ever manage. He tries incredibly hard, earning the admiration of his doubters whether he accomplishes it or not.

12th August

Prompt

Would like to meet

Quick exercise

At random pick two profiles from a dating website or lonely hearts column. Would these people be a good match?

Story/scene suggestion

Using two random profiles from a dating site or similar, write about the pair meeting. This doesn't have to be a date, or the result of them registering with the site, although it can be if you wish.

13th August

Prompt

Expert

Quick exercise

List a few subjects you know quite a lot about.

Story/scene suggestion

Create a character who seems to know something about almost everything.

14th August

Prompt

Friendly fall out

Quick exercise

Explain things you've fallen out with close friends over – and how you got back together, or why you didn't.

Story/scene suggestion

Write a scene where two close friends fall out, then show that while your main character still disagrees with the other's point of view or still considers they were in the wrong, they decide it's not worth losing the friendship over. How do they reconcile?

15th August

Prompt

Coded message

Quick exercise

Write messages hidden in another messages e.g. **HE**len **L**ikes **P**ies

Story/scene suggestion

Your character discovers what they believe is a code, tries to decipher it and then acts on the message he has, or believes he has, learned.

16th August

Prompt

Fingers and thumbs

Quick exercise

Describe something physical that you're bad at or find difficult.

Story/scene suggestion

Your character is unable to perform a task which they know many others manage easily. What can't they do? Why? How do they feel about this?

17th August

Prompt

The latest thing

Quick exercise

Are there things do you prefer to do by hand, even though it would be possible to use a machine or technology?

Story/scene suggestion

Your character is obliged to use modern technology to do something they've always managed to accomplish without that 'advantage'. Do they embrace the change or resent it?

18th August

Prompt

Too good to be true

Quick exercise

Have you ever come across a deal, or been made an offer, that seemed too good to be true?

Story/scene suggestion

Your character accepts an offer that others have warned her is too good to be true.

19th August

Prompt

Teacher's pet

Quick exercise

List everything you can remember about your favourite teacher from school, including their appearance, what they taught you and how that's helped in your life.

Story/scene suggestion

Write a scene where someone has had some kind of success (major or minor) then meets an old teacher and realises they were at least partly responsible.

20th August

Prompt

Well remembered

Quick exercise

What would you like to be remembered for?

Story/scene suggestion

Your character will soon be dead, or is leaving an area or job. They wish to be remembered in a certain way. What do they do to help ensure that's the case?

21st August

Prompt

Failed

Quick exercise

What have you failed at?

Story/scene suggestion

Your character is faced with a situation in which they once failed. What do they do differently this time?

22nd August

Prompt

Phone call

Quick exercise

List things you've been doing when your phone rang and note whether you answered or not.

Story/scene suggestion

Your character is expecting, or hoping for, a really important call, but they're in a situation where they're not supposed to use their phone.

23rd August

Prompt

For me?

Quick exercise

Describe a time when you where sent or given something, informed of good news, praised or congratulated – but weren't entirely sure you were the intended or rightful recipient.

Story/scene suggestion

Your character is sent an anonymous gift, or congratulatory message, she suspects wasn't meant for her. How does she try to trace whoever should have got it? Is she right in her assumption it wasn't intended for her?

24th August

Prompt

I wasn't there!

Quick exercise

What evidence do you leave to show you were in a place? What changes do you make to places where you've lived?

Story/scene suggestion

Your character has has spent some time in a particular place, but now wants to make it appear they've never been there. Why, and how do they go about this?

25th August

Prompt

Stop the clock

Quick exercise

If you could temporarily freeze time for everyone and everything but you, what would you do?

Story/scene suggestion

Time has apparently stopped for your character. Is he really stuck in the present, or does it just seem that way?

26th August

Prompt

Seeing red

Quick exercise

List of everything which is, or which you associate with, the colour red.

Story/scene suggestion

Pick one colour and use it as a running theme through a piece of writing. You may either blend it into something you've already written or create something new.

27th August

Prompt

Short changed

Quick exercise

Describe a time when you didn't have enough money to pay for something you wanted or needed. (Either just not enough cash on you, or totally out of your reach financially.)

Story/scene suggestion

Your character has always been financially secure, but now he either loses all his money or is unable to access it.

28th August

Prompt

You're it!

Quick exercise

Write about a game you remember from school.

Story/scene suggestion

Your character recalls a playground incident which helps them understand or decide about something in the present.

29th August

Prompt

Main ingredients

Quick exercise

List all the things you can think of which are common to the genre you'd like to write in.

Story/scene suggestion

Create a plot using every one of these. Use any extra elements you wish.

30th August

Prompt

All change

Quick exercise

Describe a major change or turning point in your life.

Story/scene suggestion

Have your character experience a life changing event and show how they deal with it.

31st August

Prompt

As I always say

Quick exercise

Which phrases or expressions do you use regularly?

Story/scene suggestion

Your character frequently uses an expression which greatly irritates someone else. How does that person reveal this annoyance, and how does your character react?

Bonus Prompt

A few little extras

Bonus exercise

Link one of these lists of words together into sentences, using as few other words as possible –

Cantaloupe, racing, cloud, mail, list and May.

Stable, cat, fridge, zen, smart and saucy.

Modified, goat, flint, round, musket and diary.

Love, fence, escape, fire, spooky and gate.

Under, lots, family, air, garden and hedge.

Bonus story/scene suggestion

Include all the words from one, or more, of the above groups of words in a short story or poem.

1st September

Prompt

What's that face for?

Quick exercise

Lists emotions and the facial expressions associated with them.

Story/scene suggestion

Your character is watching somebody making a phone call. Their expressions don't match what they're saying.

2nd September

Prompt

Starring role

Quick exercise

Describe an event that was hugely important to you.

Story/scene suggestion

Write about about an event which was important to you (fictionalising any aspects you wish). Tell it from the viewpoint of someone who seemed to have a minor role, but make it significant for them in some way.

3rd September

Prompt

Forever waiting

Quick exercise

What's the longest wait you've ever had for something (or which felt like it at the time).

Story/scene suggestion

Your character, not someone particularly patient, is waiting for something which it seems will never materialise or occur. What is it, how does he feel about the delay and will it be worth the wait?

4th September

Prompt

Flower power

Quick exercise

Compare and contrast a daisy and a holly bush.

Story/scene suggestion

Chose two very different plants and write about them as though they were people interacting in some way.

5th September

Prompt

Nothing changes

Quick exercise

What things have you done or gone through which ultimately produced no, or little, change?

Story/scene suggestion

Have your character go on a journey, physically not ending where they started, yet in a the same place mentally, emotionally or otherwise not having changed as might have been expected.

6th September

Prompt

As a result of mistakenly identifying the Crab Nebula in 1758, Charles Messier began listing astronomical objects in the now famous Messier Catalogue.

Quick exercise

When has a mistake led to you doing a lot of work?

Story/scene suggestion

Your character makes a mistake, which could have been quickly rectified had he owned up and/or acted immediately. Instead he's tried to hide either the error or his part in it and as a result, the situation is now far worse.

7th September

Prompt

Caught on film

Quick exercise

When have you ever been photographed, filmed or recorded? Has it ever happened without you being aware of it at the time?

Story/scene suggestion

Your character is watching TV and unexpectedly sees themselves, or someone they know. What's the programme, and why is footage of this person included?

8th September

Prompt

There was a young man ...

Quick exercise

Write a limerick, beginning – There was a writer called (insert your name). Add or delete words as required to suit the number of syllables in your name. If in a group, write one about the person to your left.

Story/scene suggestion

Your character frequently creates verses and rhymes about friends and family. When asked to sign cards, guests books, etc. they seem able to effortlessly produce something apt (or which they think is suitable).

9th September

Prompt

It takes two

Quick exercise

Write three sentences, with to, too and two used correctly in each. If you're in any doubt, look up how to use them first.

Story/scene suggestion

Join the sentences created in the above exercise together (along with as many others as you wish) to form a story.

10th September

Prompt

Back and forth

Quick exercise

Imagine someone from 500 years ago could see their hometown now, which happens to be where you currently live. What will surprise them? What will seem familiar?

Story/scene suggestion

Send yourself back in time to any period of history you choose and witness any event you wish. Describe the scene, including details such as what people eat and wear, and how they behave and speak. Mention any landmarks which present day readers might recognise.

11th September

Prompt

Boiling point

Quick exercise

Describe being far too hot.

Story/scene suggestion

Your character is too hot, or too cold. Why, and what do they do about it?

12th September

Prompt

Fame at last

Quick exercise

Imagine there's a picture of you in a magazine or newspaper. Which publication is it most likely to be in and why would you be featured?

Story/scene suggestion

Your character longs for fame and makes numerous attempts to get their photo into a daily newspaper. When it finally happens, the result is nothing like they'd imagined. What's happened and has it altered their wish to be famous?

13th September

Prompt

Friday the 13th

Quick exercise

Would you feel uncomfortable scheduling an important event for Friday the 13th, booking into room 13, being the 13th person at dinner, etc.?

Story/scene suggestion

Your character once had a bad experience on a Friday the 13th and now is very unwilling to do anything which could possibly go wrong on that day. How does she spend her time?

14th September

Prompt

Totally true

Quick exercise

Find a real news story. Rewrite it, making it sound as unbelievable as possible, whilst changing the facts as little as possible – ideally not at all.

Story/scene suggestion

Switch on the news. Regional, national or global. Incorporate one of the events into a piece of fiction, using as many real details as possible.

15th September

Prompt

Law and order

Quick exercise

If you could bring in one new law, or abolish an existing one, what would it be?

Story/scene suggestion

Your character is creating laws, rules or orders. Who does she expect to obey them?

16th September

Prompt

Rumour has it

Quick exercise

Have you ever passed on a rumour, or shared a social media post, without first checking it was true?

Story/scene suggestion

Your character started an unfounded rumour, which she now regrets, but it's already spread far beyond her control. Why did she start it and what is she going to do about it now?

17th September

Prompt

Tough paper round

Quick exercise

Describe your first ever job or a chore you were expected to do regularly. What do you now do which is most similar?

Story/scene suggestion

A character has had the exact same job their whole life. What is it and why have they never done anything else?

18th September

Prompt

That's how it all started

Quick exercise

Note down some of the ways you, your friends, and family, have met their partners.

Story/scene suggestion

Have two characters meet in a way that you, or someone you know, met their partner. This is to be a piece of fiction, not a real account with the names changed.

19th September

Prompt

Shipwreck

Quick exercise

You're on a ship which is sinking. You have a place on a lifeboat and can bring whatever you can carry from the ship. What would you take?

Story/scene suggestion

Your character is in a lifeboat, with others, somewhere very remote. He expects to be rescued but believes this might take three days. There's just enough food and water to last that length of time and some people have brought a few personal possessions with them. Describe how they pass the time until they see a rescue boat.

20th September

Prompt

In the beginning

Quick exercise

Write five gripping opening sentences.

Story/scene suggestion

Chose your favourite and write the opening scene (and then the entire rest of the story!).

21st September

Prompt

Agony aunt

Quick exercise

Make up a letter which might appear on a magazine (not necessarily woman's magazine) problem page.

Story/scene suggestion

Find a magazine with problem pages, or somewhere else people ask for advice, and give that situation to one of your characters. It doesn't have to be a relationship or medical problem, although it could be.

22nd September

Prompt

Season's greetings

Quick exercise

List things which are associated with a particular time of year.

Story/scene suggestion

Your character does something at what many people would consider to be the wrong time of year. What? Why?

23rd September

Prompt

Great timing

Quick exercise

Describe situations you've been in where something good happened because of the time you arrived, or the timing of something you did, meant it had an especially good result.

Story/scene suggestion

Your character arrives for an event and either the time of their arrival, or the timing of an incident, is very fortuitous. What happens?

24th September

Prompt

I should have said ...

Quick exercise

When have you come up with the perfect response or answer just too late?

Story/scene suggestion

Your character is in a recurring situation (perhaps her job) and has gradually found good answers or witty comebacks to things she's asked, or which are said.

25th September

Prompt

Light speed

Quick exercise

What's the fastest you've ever travelled, or which felt so at the time?

Story/scene suggestion

Your character feels as though they're travelling at incredible speed towards something, physically or metaphorically. Are they impatient to complete the journey, or would they like to slow it down?

26th September

Prompt

Hypnotic

Quick exercise

Describe being hypnotised, mesmerised, or spellbound.

Story/scene suggestion

Your character wakes up and is certain they've been hypnotised. What makes them think that?

27th September

Prompt

Trust issues

Quick exercise

What makes you trust and distrust people?

Story/scene suggestion

Your main character is untrustworthy. Show this through their behaviour and dialogue without they, or another character, actually saying that's the case.

28th September
Prompt

Safety in numbers?

Quick exercise

What makes you feel safe?

Story/scene suggestion

Your character is about to do something potentially unsafe. How do they either minimise the risks and/or give themselves the courage to go ahead?

29th September
Prompt

Shopping lists

Quick exercise

Write a list of the things you bought, or would like to have bought, the first time you were old enough to spend money, and at roughly ten year intervals (or at milestone events) since.

Story/scene suggestion

Show how a character's life changes through the items on their shopping list.

30th September
Prompt

What goes around

Quick exercise

What items have you owned which were previously the property of someone else and/or which you've passed on to another person?

Story/scene suggestion

Write about an item being passed from character to character, showing their varying reactions to it and/or how it impacts on their lives.

1st October

Prompt

Am I being watched?

Quick exercise

List how many times you're potentially seen by others, caught on CCTV, your image is reflected, etc. in a typical day.

Story/scene suggestion

Your character believes they're the target of deliberate surveillance. Why do they think that and are they right?

2nd October

Prompt

Ages of man

Quick exercise

If you could go back (or forward) to any age, how old would you chose to be?

Story/scene suggestion

Your character's life hit a high point at a relatively young age. They're still benefitting from, and associated with, that moment.

3rd October

Prompt

Release valve

Quick exercise

Think of someone who has angered or upset you (friend, family member, politician), write them a letter venting your feelings. Read it back the next day and then delete it.

Story/scene suggestion

Your character receives a heartfelt letter from someone they've angered or upset.

4th October

Prompt

Never saw a thing

Quick exercise

Describe seeing something you weren't intended, or hadn't wanted, to see.

Story/scene suggestion

Your character accidentally sees something they shouldn't have. As a result they now have knowledge which could be beneficial to themselves or another.

5th October

Prompt

Family photo

Quick exercise

Find a photo of people you don't know, which is, or appears to be, a family group and explain their relationship to each other and how they get on.

Story/scene suggestion

Now add or remove one person. What changes?

6th October

Prompt

Unforgettable

Quick exercise

If someone you knew decades ago was to meet you now, what would they think had changed and what stayed the same?

Story/scene suggestion

A character meets someone and suspects he knew them a long time ago. Explain describe what makes him think it's the same person and how he might try to find out if the's right. He can ask outright, but should try other methods first.

7th October

Prompt

Every day is a school day

Quick exercise

Describe a time you've had someone explain something to you.

Story/scene suggestion

Your character doesn't know, or can't understand, something that's common knowledge to most of those around him. Who explains it to him?

8th October

Prompt

Someone was here

Quick exercise

Have you ever returned to a room and thought, or known, someone else had been in since you left?

Story/scene suggestion

Nobody had reason to go into your character's home or room since she left it, but she's certain someone has.

9th October

Prompt

A dog's life

Quick exercise

Describe life for your dog (or other pet) or what it would be like to be your dog, if you had one.

Story/scene suggestion

Write a scene which would be very dramatic and emotional for the humans involved, but tell it from the point of view of any animal who is present.

10th October

<u>Prompt</u>

Super power

<u>Quick exercise</u>

What's the nearest you have to a super power?

<u>Story/scene suggestion</u>

You've developed the super power of your choice. What is it? Do you use it openly, or in disguise?

11th October

<u>Prompt</u>

Bad habits

<u>Quick exercise</u>

What are your bad habits?

<u>Story/scene suggestion</u>

Your character has a bad habit that they're trying to break. What do they do and does it make them a better/happier person overall?

12th October

<u>Prompt</u>

Praise indeed!

<u>Quick exercise</u>

When have you ever received praise for anything you've done? Including anything verbal, written or expressed in other way e.g. by giving you a gift, hug or pay rise.

<u>Story/scene suggestion</u>

Your character is having a bad day (or year) until she receives some kind of praise or thanks. This makes her determined to be worthy of future praise.

13th October

Prompt

Silence is golden

Quick exercise

If you could select some sounds never to hear again, which would they be?

Story/scene suggestion

There's a sound your character very much wants to hear. How does he attempt to do so?

14th October

Prompt

Mercury in retrograde

Quick exercise

Find horoscopes in the paper or online and write similar ones for the next day.

Story/scene suggestion

Your character reads their horoscope and acts on it – either because she believes it's true or to prove it's rubbish. What happens?

15th October

Prompt

New and improved

Quick exercise

List some of the words and phrases used in advertising to encourage people to buy a product.

Story/scene suggestion

Your character is writing advertising copy or slogans for a very dull product and attempting to make it sounds exciting or glamorous.

16th October

Prompt

In memoriam

Quick exercise

Imagine you could know exactly what people thought of you. Would you want that knowledge?

Story/scene suggestion

Write your character's obituary and then let them read it (before or after death!).

17th October

Prompt

Gets it from his dad

Quick exercise

What trait have you inherited, or learned, from a family member or other person close to you?

Story/scene suggestion

Your character notices a characteristic in a younger family member, which they either greatly admire or strongly dislike. They begin to realise they're the likely inspiration for, or cause of, this behaviour.

18th October

Prompt

He's behind you!

Quick exercise

If you were following someone, what steps would you take to avoid them realising you were interested in them?

Story/scene suggestion

Your character suspects they're being followed. After checking this is really the case, they either try to lose the follower, or deliberately lead them on a wild goose chase.

19th October

Prompt

I need it

Quick exercise

Describe a 'must have' item you craved as a child. How did you feel when you got it or realised you'd never own one?

Story/scene suggestion

There was something your character wanted as a child, but never got. They now consider this to be a good thing.

20th October

Prompt

Totally useless

Quick exercise

Write a letter of complaint for a real or imaginary product defect.

Story/scene suggestion

Your character is always complaining about things either greatly exaggerating the problem, or making things up, in the hope of getting free replacements, refunds or compensation. How does this backfire?

21st October

Prompt

Top secret

Quick exercise

When have you kept a secret?

Story/scene suggestion

Your character is asked to keep an important secret. They do, even when they begin to wonder if that's really the thing best for the person who shared the confidence.

22nd October

Prompt

Poetic licence

Quick exercise

When is it OK to say something that isn't strictly true? Or if you feel that can never be right, explain why.

Story/scene suggestion

Your character always tells the truth, even when people don't want to hear it, and he could have remained silent.

23rd October

Prompt

Desirable residence

Quick exercise

Look online, or visit an estate agent's, to get the details of a house for sale and describe the circumstances which might result in your living there.

Story/scene suggestion

Your character has a change of circumstances and will soon move into a home very different from their present one. Describe them viewing potential properties.

24th October

Prompt

Favourite foods

Quick exercise

List foods which you enjoy at least partly because of memories or associations.

Story/scene suggestion

Your character tries to recreate a meal which had special associations for another person. Do they get the food right and did the attempt have the desired result?

25th October

Prompt

Impulse buys

Quick exercise

What have you bought without thinking it through? Was that a good or bad decision?

Story/scene suggestion

Your character makes an impulsive purchase which has big impact on his life.

26th October

Prompt

Child's play

Quick exercise

Describe someone you did in your childhood, but haven't done since.

Story/scene suggestion

Your character is behaving in a childlike manner. What are they doing and why?

27th October

Prompt

Miss Spell

Quick exercise

When have you got somebody's name wrong?

Story/scene suggestion

Your character's name is unusual, so sometimes misspelled or mispronounced until she puts people right. However one character seems to deliberately get it wrong all of the time, even 'correcting' those who are saying it properly.

28th October

Prompt

Suspicious behaviour

Quick exercise

When have you done something innocent which may have appeared suspicious to an onlooker, or witnessed apparently suspicious behaviour?

Story/scene suggestion

Your character has a good reason for doing something which she's aware appears suspicious to others. Does she explain her actions? Do others challenge her?

29th October

Prompt

Joyful sound

Quick exercise

What are the happiest sounds you can think of?

Story/scene suggestion

A your character hears something which makes her happy. Why does that particular sound bring her joy?

30th October

Prompt

Heads or tails?

Quick exercise

Describe something which is the result of random chance.

Story/scene suggestion

Your character does, or is involved in, something most people consider the result of random chance. He believes that there's a way to predict or influence whatever it is.

31st October

Prompt

Haunting

Quick exercise

Have you ever seen a ghost or experienced anything spooky?

Story/scene suggestion

Your character meets someone who is, or she believed to be, dead.

Bonus Prompt

Even more

Bonus exercise

Link one of these lists of words together into sentences, using as few other words as possible –

Sausage, yesterday, resist, what, over and smile.

Joint, burn, baby, warmer, Queen and November.

Prize, council, horse, free delivery, bridge and spot.

Untidy, third, borough, arts, erased and job.

Window, character, application, bin and photo.

Bonus story/scene suggestion

Include all the words from one, or more, of the above groups of words in a short story or poem.

1st November
Prompt

Orange

Quick exercise

Describe an orange in as much detail as possible without using the words orange or fruit.

Story/scene suggestion

Your character has forgotten the name of something but doesn't wish to admit the fact. Make him talk about the thing in question.

2nd November
Prompt

The ideal candidate

Quick exercise

Describe a job interview or other time you've attempted to persuade someone of your worth.

Story/scene suggestion

Your character is applying for a job they either never wanted, or which they come to realise they don't want.

3rd November
Prompt

Fire!

Quick exercise

Give a brief description of all they types of real fire and flame you've seen, concentrating on their impact on you, rather than straightforward description.

Story/scene suggestion

A character sees a destructive fire at first hand and considers it to be at least partly positive.

4th November

Prompt

Appearances are deceptive

Quick exercise

Do you know anyone whose appearance is at odds with what they're really like?

Story/scene suggestion

Write about two characters who look similar, but are otherwise very different.

5th November

Prompt

Fireworks

Quick exercise

At firework display what would you see, hear, smell, taste, and feel?

Story/scene suggestion

Write about two neighbours. One hates fireworks. The other, who is unaware of this dislike/fear, is letting them off in their garden for a very special reason initially unknown to the neighbour. They get together and learn of the other person's feelings and reasons.

6th November

Prompt

Hurry!

Quick exercise

Describe the last thing you did in a hurry.

Story/scene suggestion

Have your character walking to a café and eating a sandwich first when they have time to kill, then when in a hurry. Try to show the reader, through the way you describe the action, which is which rather than telling them.

7th November

Prompt

The kindest cut

Quick exercise

Find a story or other piece of writing you were quite happy with and reduce it by ten percent.*

Story/scene suggestion

Bring the above piece back to it's original word count by adding in an extra thread, introducing a theme, or including a twist (or extra twist) or surprise at the end.*

*If you're a very new writer, do one of the 'bonus' exercise I've snuck onto the end of some months, and come back to this one later.

8th November

Prompt

Ooops!

Quick exercise

Write about a mistake you've made.

Story/scene suggestion

Your character once made a mistake and is now determined never to repeat it. Are they successful? Do they make other mistakes instead?

9th November

Prompt

A quick chat

Quick exercise

Recall a recent conversation and write down as accurately as possible everything you both said – including any ums, ahs and clichés.

Story/scene suggestion

Write a conversation in which one person is unwilling to state any opinions without first learning what the other person thinks.

10th November

<u>Prompt</u>

Congratulations!

<u>Quick exercise</u>

You have something to celebrate. Who do you hope to get a card or greeting from, and what kind of party or celebration, if any, would you like?

<u>Story/scene suggestion</u>

Your character has something to celebrate. She thought she had a good idea exactly who she'd hear from and what would happen, but the day is very different from the one she'd anticipated.

11th November

<u>Prompt</u>

Once upon a time

<u>Quick exercise</u>

Rewrite a fairytale as though writing a factual report set in the present.

<u>Story/scene suggestion</u>

Your character has been asked to investigate something and write a report. What they see or uncover seems more like fantasy than reality, so they leave out, or minimise, some aspects in order to make it more believable.

12th November

<u>Prompt</u>

Handmade

<u>Quick exercise</u>

What's the first thing you can recall ever having made?

<u>Story/scene suggestion</u>

Your character makes something for a loved one. What is it, how talented are they, and how is the gift received?

13th November

Prompt

Language of flowers

Quick exercise

List some types of flowers, or flower arrangements/uses, adding any associations they have for you.

Story/scene suggestion

Your character is trying to select flowers to convey a precise message. What is it they're hoping to get across and which flowers or style of arrangement do they opt for?

14th November

Prompt

Suppressed laughter

Quick exercise

Explain a situation where you've tried not to laugh.

Story/scene suggestion

Your character is amused either at something she feels she can't admit to finding funny, or something unconnected to what's going on immediately around her, and so tries to disguise her amusement.

15th November

Prompt

Things can only get better

Quick exercise

Describe a potentially bad situation which turned out better than you'd expected.

Story/scene suggestion

Your character is dreading something, tries to get out of it, and ends up glad he went through with it.

16th November

Prompt

It's traditional

Quick exercise

What traditions or rituals do you, your friends or family observe which aren't common among other groups?

Story/scene suggestion

Your character has always observed a tradition or ritual along with those around them. Although they now live somewhere else, where this practise isn't observed, they wish to continue. How do they attempt to get others to join in?

17th November

Prompt

First aid

Quick exercise

If you came across an injured person, in what way would you be of most help?

Story/scene suggestion

Your character is the first on the scene at an accident. What do they do?

18th November

Prompt

Vaguely familiar

Quick exercise

Describe a location you know well, but change one important detail so another person familiar with the area wouldn't be sure it was the same place.

Story/scene suggestion

Your character goes somewhere familiar and something has changed. What? Why? Does it matter to them?

19th November

Prompt

A girlie girl

Quick exercise

List some behaviours and actions which are stereotypically feminine.

Story/scene suggestion

Write about a male character in such a way that the reader will initially think they're female (or vice versa) and then add a detail which reveals the truth.

20th November

Prompt

Should have known what would happen

Quick exercise

When have you done, or attempted something you knew might not go well, or probably wasn't a good idea, even before you started?

Story/scene suggestion

Your character is expected to do something they are sure will be a disaster. Can they get out of it?

21st November

Prompt

Keeping up with the Joneses

Quick exercise

Have you ever done something more to impress others than because it's what you really wanted to do?

Story/scene suggestion

Your character is obsessed with what others think of them and always trying to impress, even if that means doing things they'd otherwise far rather not attempt.

22nd November

Prompt

Differing points of view

Quick exercise

Write a few lines in each of 1st person (I), 2nd person (You) and 3rd person (He/she/they/it).

Story/scene suggestion

Write a dramatic scene in first person from one character's point of view, then rewrite it from another character's point of view (in 1st, 2nd or 3rd person). Have subtle differences between each version which indicate that at least one of them is lying or trying to mislead the reader.

23rd November

Prompt

Still waiting

Quick exercise

When have you waited for someone who didn't show up, or an event which didn't happen?

Story/scene suggestion

Your character has agreed to a meeting, which isn't convenient to them. They go to some trouble in order to get there, but the other person doesn't show up.

24th November

Prompt

Rule breaker

Quick exercise

When have you deliberately, or accidentally, broken a rule?

Story/scene suggestion

Your character is constantly breaking rules. They expect to be caught, but so far they've got away with it.

25th November

Prompt

Friendly face

Quick exercise

When have you been friendly to someone you didn't particularly like?

Story/scene suggestion

Your character has to be pleasant to, or gain the trust of a person or people they really dislike, for the benefit of someone else they care about. How do they do this?

26th November

Prompt

Talking quietly

Quick exercise

Think of words, phrases or situations to show a person is talking quietly.

Story/scene suggestion

Your character always speaks very softly, yet still manages to get people to listen to him.

27th November

Prompt

It's a sign!

Quick exercise

When have you experienced what you felt was a supernatural, spiritual or religious sign, or a message from another time or dimension?

Story/scene suggestion

Your character keeps receiving what seem to be signs from the spirit world. At first they're sceptical and refuse to act on them, but the messages become clearer, more detailed and increasingly insistent.

28th November

<u>Prompt</u>

Nip and tuck

<u>Quick exercise</u>

You're offered free cosmetic surgery, a makeover, hair cut and wardrobe of new clothes. What's one aspect of your appearance you definitely wouldn't change?

<u>Story/scene suggestion</u>

Your character goes through something which greatly alters their appearance, for the better or worse. What happens and how does it change their life?

29th November

<u>Prompt</u>

Voice from the past

<u>Quick exercise</u>

Which one person, who is no longer living, would you like to be able to talk to?

<u>Story/scene suggestion</u>

Your character asks a dead person, or their image, or representation, for help and gets the answers they need.

30th November

<u>Prompt</u>

News to me

<u>Quick exercise</u>

When have you missed hearing a piece of news until after most other people knew?

<u>Story/scene suggestion</u>

There's a big announcement which your character somehow misses hearing about. No one tells her as they assume she will know.

1st December
Prompt

Giving up

Quick exercise

Have you ever given up doing something, broken a bad habit, or made a change to your routine?

Story/scene suggestion

Your character wishes, or has no choice but, to give up doing something that's been part of their life for a long time.

2nd December
Prompt

Ear worm

Quick exercise

What song or phrase have you ever had stuck in your head? (Sorry – you probably have it again now.)

Story/scene suggestion

Your character keeps hearing the same piece of music or phrase and this becomes significant to the story.

3rd December
Prompt

What's in a name?

Quick exercise

Who do you know who perfectly suits their name?

Story/scene suggestion

Write a story where the characters' names reflect their appearance or personality in some way.

4th December

Prompt

Lifelike

Quick exercise

You suspect your partner or family member has been replaced with a robot or alien. What clues would you pick up on?

Story/scene suggestion

There's a robot version of you. What makes people realise it isn't the genuine article?

5th December

Prompt

Repent at leisure

Quick exercise

When have you rushed into making a big decision? Did it work out well?

Story/scene suggestion

Your character is incredibly impulsive and keeps making big decisions without stopping to think. Write about them from another character's point of view.

6th December

Prompt

Lost property

Quick exercise

Describe losing something important or of sentimental value.

Story/scene suggestion

Your character has lost something very important to them, or which they'll need to use very soon. How do they feel, what do they do to attempt to find it and are they successful?

7th December
Prompt

Comfort food

Quick exercise

Write out the recipe for a favourite dish, making it as vivid as possible by using the senses and describing the actions in detail.

Story/scene suggestion

Show a character creating a favourite recipe and bring in memories of previous times they've made it and compare with their current situation. Maybe they're teaching it to someone else, making it in a very different place, or for different people than they'd previously have thought possible.

8th December
Prompt

A flare for fashion

Quick exercise

Describe the first fashionable outfit you ever wore.

Story/scene suggestion

A character wears an outfit which was once fashionable, but definitely isn't now. Why do they wear it and what do they, and others, think of it?

9th December
Prompt

Decisions, decisions

Quick exercise

What is one of the hardest decisions you've had to make?

Story/scene suggestion

Your character made an extremely difficult decision. They're now in a very similar situation. Do they make the same choice?

10th December

Prompt

Can you repeat the question?

Quick exercise

Describe not listening or paying attention when you should have done.

Story/scene suggestion

Your character isn't paying attention when he's given some important information. What distracted him, what did he miss and what's the result?

11th December

Prompt

Not my best work

Quick exercise

Write something deliberately awful and full of errors. Try to avoid making those same errors in future, unless doing it on purpose.

Story/scene suggestion

Your character deliberately makes a bad job of something they're usually good at.

12th December

Prompt

Why can't people ...?

Quick exercise

List a few things which you wish everyone did automatically, but which apparently is a special skill possessed by a select few (e.g. replacing a toilet roll after using the last sheet).

Story/scene suggestion

Write a story in which a character finally learns to do something they've been repeatedly reminded about.

13th December

Prompt

Bystander

Quick exercise

Describe an event that was important to someone else, but in which you had a very minor role.

Story/scene suggestion

Your character expects to be the centre of attention at an event, but gets eclipsed by someone else.

14th December

Prompt

That's weird

Quick exercise

Describe doing something that's perfectly sensible, but would look peculiar to anyone who saw it out of context or didn't know the full story.

Story/scene suggestion

Your character hears people discussing someone's odd behaviour and realises exactly what they were doing and why. She could explain, but decides not to.

15th December

Prompt

Four walls

Quick exercise

Write about events in a home which make it clear in which room they're happening, without actually saying 'bathroom', 'kitchen,' etc.

Story/scene suggestion

Your character is asked to describe a room they claim to have been in. They do, but are so vague it could be the same kind of room in almost any home.

16th December

Prompt

It's for charity

Quick exercise

What was the last, or most interesting, time you did something for charity or other good cause and why do you support that particular organisation?

Story/scene suggestion

Your character is attempting to do something for others and finding it difficult to get the support she needs. What does she do to make someone with influence aware of the problem?

17th December

Prompt

Good God

Quick exercise

List all the religions and belief systems you can think of, along with a few lines to describe their principles (if you know).

Story/scene suggestion

Two characters who have very different beliefs, or one with a strong religious faith, and one with none, discover that they do believe the same about some aspects of life.

18th December

Prompt

Are you OK?

Quick exercise

Describe either seeing someone in distress and helping comfort them, or being comforted yourself.

Story/scene suggestion

Your character comes to the aid of someone in distress. This act leads to a lasting friendship or relationship.

19th December

<u>Prompt</u>

Spam!

<u>Quick exercise</u>

Read a spam (unsolicited and unwanted) email or text, or listen to a spam phone call and describe the person responsible.

<u>Story/scene suggestion</u>

Your character receives unwelcome mail or calls and then discovers the person creating it has a valid or understandable reason for doing so.

20th December

<u>Prompt</u>

White lies

<u>Quick exercise</u>

When have you lied, or kept something hidden, to make life easier for yourself or another?

<u>Story/scene suggestion</u>

Your character lied to try to help someone he cares about. The other person learned the truth and now won't accept his help, even though it would greatly assist them.

21st December

<u>Prompt</u>

Bad taste

<u>Quick exercise</u>

What's your least favourite food and why?

<u>Story/scene suggestion</u>

Your character is presented with their least favourite food under circumstances in which they feel obliged to eat and pretend to enjoy it.

22nd December

Prompt

The good deed

Quick exercise

What nice things has anyone ever done for you?

Story/scene suggestion

Your character is on the receiving end of a generous act. What is it and how does it influence the rest of their day?

23rd December

Prompt

Knock knock

Quick exercise

Someone is knocking on your door – who is it likely to be?

Story/scene suggestion

Your character answers a knock on her door, certain she knows who is there, but it's someone totally unexpected.

24th December

Prompt

Needing a fix

Quick exercise

Describe something you're addicted to either physically or emotionally, or the thing you'd least like to give up. In what way do you rely on it?

Story/scene suggestion

A character is forced to give up or unable to obtain what they're addicted to. How do they feel? Do they select something else as an alternative? Sometime later they regain access to their addictive item – what do they do?

25th December

Prompt

All the trimmings

Quick exercise

Describe any large, rich or complicated meal and how you felt after eating it.

Story/scene suggestion

Your character has to eat fancy food fairly often because of their job, or social situation. Does he enjoy that aspect? What does he eat when completely free to choose?

26th December

Prompt

The end is nigh!

Quick exercise

If the world was due to end next week, what would you do?

Story/scene suggestion

Your character thinks something will end, or a person will die, and does something because of that – then the predicted event either doesn't happen, or is delayed.

27th December

Prompt

So polite

Quick exercise

List behaviours which are considered polite

Story/scene suggestion

Your character has always behaved politely, no matter what happened – until now.

28th December

Prompt

Spanner in the works

Quick exercise

Do you always use the correct tool for a job, even if it takes time and effort to locate it, or do you improvise if that seems easier or quicker?

Story/scene suggestion

Your character wants to perform a routine task, but hasn't got the usual tool to do it with. How do they get around this problem?

29th December

Prompt

Best job in the world

Quick exercise

Describe your perfect job – including hours, pay and perks.

Story/scene suggestion

Your character has what they thought would be their dream job. What is it, why did they want it, and are they as happy as they thought they'd be?

30th December

Prompt

Insomnia

Quick exercise

What do you do if you find it hard to sleep?

Story/scene suggestion

Your character is having trouble sleeping. Why? Is this usual for them?

31st December

<u>Prompt</u>
Round and round

<u>Quick exercise</u>
List things which are continuous or a repetitive cycle.

<u>Story/scene suggestion</u>
Have your character go on a journey, physically ending where they started, yet in a different place mentally, emotionally or otherwise changed.

A few reminders

- You don't have to do these prompts on the 'right' day, or in order. Feel free to skip ones which don't appeal, perhaps coming back to them later, or to do more than one in a day, or combine two into a single piece of work.
- It's fine to alter some aspects of a prompt, or of a story you've started writing, if you feel that will produce a better piece of writing.
- You do not have to write every day. You can if you have the time and inclination, but I think it would be a huge mistake to spend all your free time writing. If you do, you'll run out of things to write about – and friends to help celebrate when you achieve success with your work.
- The stories, and other pieces of writing, you create using these prompts are yours to do with exactly as you wish.

Thank you for reading this book. I hope you enjoyed it. If you did, I'd really appreciate it if you could spare the time to leave a short review on Amazon and/or Goodreads.

To learn more about my writing life, hear about new releases and get a free short ebook, news and competitions, sign up to my newsletter – subscribepage.io/ItLSNa or you can find the link on my website patsycollins.co.uk

You may also find this book of interest –

From Story Idea to Reader
(co-written with Rosemary J. Kind)

An easily accessible guide to writing fiction.

Whether brushing up your writing skills or starting out, this book will take you through the whole process from inspiration to conclusion.

Are you looking to submit your work for publication, enter a competition, or do you want to self-publish? This practical guide will help you every step of the way.

Between them, Patsy Collins and Rosemary Kind have sold hundreds of short stories, written sixteen published books and produced numerous articles for Writing Magazine and similar publications. They've both judged writing competitions and run workshops, and Rosemary has read and edited thousands of short stories and published dozens of books for other writers.

With the information, help and encouragement in this book, you too could see your work in print.

Buy it now and give your writing life a boost.

Other books by Patsy Collins

Novels

Firestarter
Escape To The Country
A Year And A Day
Paint Me A Picture
Leave Nothing But Footprints
Acting Like A Killer

Little Mallow cosy mystery series

Disguised Murder and Community Spirit in Little Mallow
Dependable Friends and Deceitful Neighbours in Little Mallow
Deadly Words and Innocent Gossip in Lille Mallow

Short story collections

Over The Garden Fence
Up The Garden Path
Through The Garden Gate
In The Garden Air
Beyond The Garden Wall

No Family Secrets
Can't Choose Your Family
Keep It In The Family
Family Feeling
Happy Families

Criminal Intent
Crime In Mind

All That Love Stuff
With Love And Kisses
Lots Of Love
Love Is The Answer

Slightly Spooky Stories I
Slightly Spooky Stories II
Slightly Spooky Stories II
Slightly Spooky Stories IV
Slightly Spooky Stories V

Just A Job
Perfect Timing
Dressed to Impress
A Way With Words
Coffee & Cake
Making A Move
Not A Drop To Drink
Days To Remember
A Clean Bill Of Health
Your Good Health

www.ingramcontent.com/pod-product-compliance
Lightning Source LLC
Chambersburg PA
CBHW071736080526
44588CB00013B/2059